Young Women's Monologues from Contemporary Plays #2

PROFESSIONAL AUDITIONS FOR ASPIRING ACTRESSES

Edited by
GERALD LEE RATLIFF

MERIWETHER PUBLISHING
A division of Pioneer Drama Service, Inc.
Denver, Colorado

Meriwether Publishing
A division of
Pioneer Drama Service, Inc.
PO Box 4267
Englewood, CO 80155

www.pioneerdrama.com

Executive editor: Theodore O. Zapel
Assistant editor: Audrey Scheck
Cover design: Jan Melvin

The Library of Congress has cataloged the paperback edition as follows:

Young women's monologues from contemporary plays #2 : professional auditions for aspiring actresses / Edited by Gerald Lee Ratliff.
     p. cm.
  ISBN 978-1-56608-153-5 (pbk.)
1. Monologues. 2. Acting--Auditions. 3. American drama--20th century. 4. English drama--20th century. I. Ratliff, Gerald Lee
  PN2080.Y73 2008
  808.82'45--dc22

                                              2008000046

                1   2   3   20   21   22

Contents

Chapter 3
Comic Mirrors: Funhouse and Fantasy

Chapter 4
Cracked Mirrors: Dark and Distorted

Chapter 5
Stained Mirrors: Pain and Sorrow 121

Chapter 6
Shattered Mirrors: Fire and Ice 155

Foreword

"Listen. This is the noise of myth.
It makes the same sound as shadow.
Can you hear it?"
— Eavan Boland, *The Journey*

Taken all together, this new collection of monologues and duo scenes weave a rich and vivid tapestry of uncommon women who confront private demons that haunt their lives. They know and understand one another's secrets but are bound to betray them to others. The strong bonds of sisterhood — forged by both female and male authors — that exist between these women help balance the tension between dreams deferred and future hopes that lie somewhere beyond the horizon. It is in the perilous journey to discover a sense of meaning and fulfillment in life that these stories celebrate life and have their most lyrical quality.

Before they can move forward, however, these characters must first confront the ghosts of their past. The journey allows them to step back in time once more and grapple with the tangled strands of their lives to let the healing begin. It's about guilt, self-punishment, and redemption. It's wildly funny, tragically sad, and yet courageous. There are moments of rueful humor and quiet reflection over roads that are not always so well traveled. The sharp observations made here ask real questions about what we believe in, what we yearn for, and what principles we wish to live by in our struggle to survive. The answers are not always what we might expect to hear.

Some may see this collection as a paean to women and a plaintiff plea for other women to tell their stories as well. Others may see this collection as a bold attempt to close the "gap" between the sexes by pointing out the *shared* basic elements of our humanity expressed here. Although these voices may, indeed, speak to all of us some of the time, and some of us all of the time, the sobering truth is that there are no clear and simple answers anymore. For some of us, the shifting tides of power and passion may not as yet afford us the scope or the depth of understanding needed to grasp the ideas and thoughts voiced in these stories for all of us.

The stories, may, however, enlarge our perspective on the issues discovered along the journey and speed the evolution of our own behavior and social thought. If we listen, if we hear, then perhaps we will also believe in the possibility of honestly and lovingly living as equals in the modern world, despite the hardships we inevitably face. Thus, the ultimate journey in this collection asks us to set our own lives on a firmer path and to live life rather than letting it live us. The collection is presented in chapter themes with brief sketches to introduce the characters and set the scene for each monologue or duologue. The high quality of the writing lends itself to classroom discussion, text analysis, and performance. The collection features well-known playwrights like Pulitzer Prize winners Arthur Miller, Wendy Wasserstein, August Wilson, and Doug Wright, as well as a host of emerging new authors whose work is sure to challenge you in both character interpretation and performance. Some of the excerpts are formal comic or dramatic texts, and some experiment with form and language. Special features are introductory chapter discussions on audition practices, text analysis principles, and rehearsal techniques. There are also a number of original, independent monologues written especially for classroom discussion and exploration in the rehearsal period.

Chapter I
Reflections in the Mirror: Audition Blueprint

> "There are two ways of spreading light: to be
> the candle or the mirror that reflects it."
> — Edith Wharton, *Vesalius in Zante*

A memorable audition performance involves much more than just understanding the text or exhibiting solid acting technique. Actors sometimes make the simple mistake of selecting audition monologues because they like them or because the monologues are well known. They forget that the goal of an audition is to demonstrate in a limited amount of time — usually three or four minutes — a vocal and physical character portrait that is honest, natural, and spontaneous. Like the image of a lit candle, they glow briefly but then flicker out in performance because they did not take the time to select more competitive audition monologues. They may not have, for example, probed beneath the lives of their fictional figures to discover the inner conflicts, hidden desires, or frustrated passions of the character. Or they were unable to reflect those character traits in a memorable audition performance. It is important to have a personal connection with your monologue and to accurately interpret the character's emotional and intellectual point of view. Look for monologues that attract your immediate identification with the character's attitude, given circumstances in the text, or reaction to the situation being described. A monologue that encourages you to act instinctively and to make bold performance choices may also indicate who you are. It is important to suit potential monologues to the posted audition call — whether the call is for a specific character, specialty character, or general character — that complements your own age, experience, and vocal or physical range. Preparing for a successful audition requires that you be familiar with standard practices and develop an audition blueprint during the rehearsal period. Most auditions call for a **prepared reading**, where you are asked to perform two contrasting memorized monologues selected from classical, Shakespeare, modern, or contemporary texts. The prepared reading is an opportunity for the director to determine your ability to clearly distinguish different character attitudes or moods — vocally as well as physically — and to evaluate your ability to phrase dialogue, interpret text, and suggest modest character development.

A **cold reading** or **directed reading** may also be part of the audition process. In a cold reading, you may be given a brief excerpt from a text and asked to perform the selection with little or no time for preparation. In a directed reading, you may be given a monologue from a text and very specific directions to follow in dialogue interpretation, vocal or physical response, and stage movement. Both the cold reading and the directed reading provide an opportunity for the director to evaluate your natural spontaneity, ability to follow direction, and improvisation skills.

Basic Practices

There are a number of basic practices to consider when you begin to review audition monologues. First, look for monologues that have one climactic moment, a series of striking turning points, and conflict (internal or external). Second, look for monologues that have a beginning, middle, and end. This simple sequence of incidents allows a character in a brief period of time to express a point of view, exhibit a sense of direction, and then pursue a course of action that is ultimately resolved in a concluding incident of some intensity. Third, look for monologues that encourage you to make performance choices that build moment-to-moment anticipation and suspense. At the same time, it may be necessary to exclude some monologues from your list of potential audition material. Learn to avoid monologues that rely on elaborate costumes, hand props, set pieces, or sound effects to visualize a character portrait. Learn to avoid monologues that are essentially narrative — monologues in which you're simply "retelling" a story rather than being a character playing an action in a specific circumstance. Learn to avoid monologues that make frequent reference to obscenities or that call for special accents or dialects.

Your initial review of monologues should focus on texts that actively engage the voice and body in mental and physical activity. It is important that the audition monologue be simple and direct so that you are playing character *actions* rather than *emotions*. The monologue should have a rising tempo or rhythm that underscores the attitude and mood of the character and should present an opportunity for movement that will help visualize the character portrait. Finally, there should not be multiple references to other characters in the monologue — just the character speaking — unless it is essential to understanding the given circumstances being described in the text.

Audition Blueprint

You will need to design an audition blueprint during the rehearsal period to enhance your competitive edge. A good starting point is to consider every performance situation — oral reports, small group discussions, public speaking events, forensic competitions — as an opportunity to cultivate poise, relaxed voice, and a body that is free of tension. The more you actively participate in these activities, the easier it will be to design an audition blueprint that pays close attention to vocal variety, ease of movement, and emotional honesty. Gaining frequent experience in a variety of performance situations will also prepare you to address any stage fright that may accompany an audition. Stage fright is a natural symptom of pounding heart, sweaty palms, and knocking knees that often affects the voice and body in a performance situation. Of course, we all experience these symptoms of anxiety and nervousness when facing an audience — whether as actors, politicians, dancers, teachers, salespersons, or singers. Stage fright, however, can be a positive experience which, when harnessed, gives a performance animation and vitality. For a more detailed discussion of stage fright and strategies available to combat its basic symptoms, please see the Chapter 2 discussion of vocal and physical relaxation exercises. In order to become familiar with some basic audition expectations, review the following guidelines before developing your own audition blueprint. Although you will learn more about these practices through actual experience, the following guidelines should serve as a model in the rehearsal period. Remember that the first twenty-five seconds of a monologue are the most crucial in terms of indicating your potential range of emotional, physical, and vocal qualities. At the same time, the last twenty-five seconds may be just as crucial to reinforce character development through subtle shifts in vocal tone and stage movement. That is why it is important to design an audition blueprint that mirrors the **stage world** of your monologue character rather than simply "acting" in an empty room or on a bare stage.

Audition Attitude

Cultivate a positive attitude through careful preparation and rehearsal. There may be a **silent listener** in your monologue — another character — so direct your voice, facial expressions, and body language *into* the audience rather than at an imaginary character on-stage. Although the monologue may not always reflect your true age, gender, or race, do not play age — play yourself and act in the present tense even if the monologue is describing past events. Remember that gestures, posture, and movement are the physical signature of a character portrait, so be fluid and precise in your performance choices. A positive audition attitude suggests a free-spirited actor, with a hint of uninhibited abandon and risk-taking, who exhibits spontaneous reactions in framing a character portrait.

Audition Choices

It is important to make a performance choice for your monologue character. Making the choice is more important than making the *right* choice. Performance choices should be made only after you have analyzed the text to identify the (a) incident being described, (b) apparent conflict, (c) language and word choices, (d) emotional moments, and (e) character's present state of mind. You may discover, for example, that a character's physical characteristics will limit performance opportunities for excessive movement. Or you may decide that a character's primary objective in the text resembles the metaphor "life is meaningless" and lends itself to stage business such as randomly knitting a scarf or aimlessly stroking a photograph album. No matter what the final performance choices may be, they should have surfaced in an analysis of the text and be appropriate for the character portrait.

Audition Time

Always arrive early for an audition; *never* arrive late! Think of the audition as an appointment and be punctual. Avoid the tendency to socialize at an audition; show respect for fellow actors by keeping conversation and noise to a minimum. Review the text or warm-up with vocal and physical relaxation exercises while waiting to have your name called. You should also respect the time limit set for each actor and for the monologue performance. In the rehearsal period, it may be necessary to time your monologue performance and make appropriate cuts in the text to meet the announced time limit. As a general rule of thumb, monologue introductions should be thirty seconds or less, and a single monologue should be between two and three minutes unless otherwise indicated in the audition notice. Avoid alcohol, cigarettes, caffeine, or other stimulants that might disrupt your concentration and focus prior to an audition.

Audition Audience

It is *not* a good idea to use specific individuals in the audience to represent the characters you may be addressing. This approach may be very uncomfortable for audience members and may also be distracting for you if the audience members become disinterested in your performance. The role of **offstage focus**, however, may be very useful in an audition setting. Offstage focus, or character placement out of the playing space, places the location of characters and incidents on a straight or angled line slightly above the heads of the audience. Offstage focus also places the actor in a full-front, presentational position and directs striking facial expressions, subtle physical movements, and colorful vocal responses toward the listeners. Do not lose your concentration if members of the audience look down to write notes or turn to whisper to each other. They may be evaluators who are actually writing positive comments or sharing favorable opinions on your audition skills.

Audition Makeup

Light street makeup or a warm bronzer is appropriate for auditions. Women sometimes wear their hair up for classical monologues; hair should always be kept away from the face so expressions may be seen clearly. If you have long hair, pull it back so it doesn't fall in your face while performing. Do not rely on elaborate accessories such as wigs or hair extensions that might be distracting. Avoid wearing platform shoes, flip-flops, or high heels that tend to make movement awkward or unnatural. The role of makeup in an audition is to accent facial expressions with a hint of color. You would not, for example, wear white clown makeup to audition for the master of ceremonies in *Cabaret* or a mask to suggest one of the animals in *The Lion King*.

Audition Wardrobe

An appropriate wardrobe is simple and reflects the attitude and mood of the monologue character. The wardrobe should be carefully selected in terms of cut, style, and color to enhance physical dimensions. Warm and soft colors that complement the eyes and skin tone are particularly effective. If you are auditioning two contrasting monologues, dress in neutral colors and let the performance choices in each monologue suggest subtle differences in the character portraits. Avoid any tendency to wear a theatrical costume to an audition, and focus on traditional designer principles of line, texture, and modest ornament. Tight jeans, short skirts, and plunging necklines are inappropriate for an audition. Do not wear leotards or knee boots because you are playing Viola disguised as a young man in Shakespeare's *Twelfth Night.* Wearing comfortable clothes and shoes that permit easy, fluid movement is always a good audition idea. Remember that a carefully selected wardrobe can suggest the monologue character's lifestyle or sense of self.

Audition Props

Hand props should be limited to specific objects that are a logical extension of the monologue character. Some examples might include Laura's miniature glass unicorn in Tennessee Williams' *The Glass Menagerie* or Sister Rita's rosary beads in Milan Stitt's *The Runner Stumbles.* If you choose to use a hand prop, it should be clearly suggested in the text and be small enough to handle easily — like a photograph, glasses, handkerchief, or a letter in a coat pocket. Do not litter the stage with an assortment of hand props that may later become part of your audition performance. Remember that an audition is never about props or other theatrical accessories. An audition is about you and how to fill an empty space using yourself as a prop!

Audition Space

Try to rehearse in the audition space before the scheduled appointment day to explore the vocal and physical demands of the playing area. Pay special attention to size, entrance and exit doorways, seating arrangement, and acoustics. Familiarity with the audition space should help you experience a more comfortable and relaxed atmosphere in which to execute fluid movement and exhibit a vibrant vocal quality in performance. Rehearsal in the audition space will also help you combat any anxiety and tension associated with performing in an unfamiliar environment. If you are unable to gain prior access to the audition space, rehearse in a number of different staging areas to anticipate auditions that might be held in classrooms, dance studios, music halls, community centers, cafeterias, rehearsal rooms, or on traditional theatre stages.

Audition Accents

Auditions are most frequently performed in standard American speech that is free of vocal regionalism, colloquialism, or distracting speech patterns. Use character accents only if they can be voiced with accuracy and authenticity. Cultivate a working catalog of traditional audition accents like British, Cockney, German, Italian, New York (Brooklyn), Southern American, Spanish, Oriental, Gypsy, and Midwestern. It may be useful to purchase accent tapes, learn the phonetic alphabet, or view film and television clips that feature ethnic accents to cultivate skills in dialect accuracy.

Audition Business

The role of stage business to advance the storyline of the text, or to provide additional visual clues in character development, is limited in an audition. Effective stage business in an audition establishes a sense of character familiarity. It may also be used to indicate a character's attitude and mood. Initial hints of stage business should be revealed in the text or in the dialog of what other stage figures may say about a character. Some of the more common uses of stage business involve handling small props, adjusting articles of clothing, or exhibiting character habits or mannerisms like cracking the knuckles or scratching the head.

Audition Staging

In staging the monologue you should anticipate a limited number of set pieces — perhaps a single chair, stool, and small table. Do not consider staging that includes elaborate decoration, mood lighting, special effects, or sound. Stage blocking — or character movement in the playing space — should be limited to focus attention on the character's action, attitude, and intention in the selected text. What is most important in staging is *placement* in the playing space. Set up the space so you are facing the audience, and be careful not to deliver the entire monologue in profile. Place imaginary characters offstage left or right, and do not look down at the stage floor while performing. Unless you have a specific reason to do otherwise, perform the monologue in the center of the playing space and move downstage left or right as appropriate. Do not back up, turn around, or move upstage unless the text suggests such movement.

Audition Movement

Although stage movement plays a significant role in fleshing-out character portraits in full-length playscripts, it is not likely to have an immediate impact on an abbreviated monologue audition. You should, however, explore subtle movement opportunities in the rehearsal period that help define the character portrait in terms of gesture, posture, or stance. Remember that character intention or motivation can also be revealed by the manner in which a character sits, stands, or walks. A good audition blueprint maintains a careful balance between movement that punctuates character action or underlines character attitude and movement that accentuates the tempo or rhythm of the performance.

Audition Entrance/Exit

An entrance and an exit are also significant elements in a monologue audition and need to be executed with style. As soon as you enter, seize the space! Walk with an air of self-confidence and make direct eye contact with the audience. If you need to move a chair to set up the playing space, do so quickly and quietly. Go directly to center stage to introduce yourself and your monologue selections. Don't forget to pause before and after your introduction. At the end of the audition, pause again to hold the monologue's climactic moment or concluding line. Then simply say, "Thank you," and exit with the same air of self-confidence and eye contact that marked your entrance. Do not chat, shake hands, or mingle with the audience. Do not comment on your performance, especially to offer apologies or make excuses. Be prepared, if you are asked to remain behind for a brief interview, to respond to an improvised situation, or to interpret a brief text for a cold or directed reading.

Audition Warm-Up

Plan to arrive at least forty-five minutes in advance of the scheduled audition time to warm-up your voice and body. Vocal and physical relaxation exercises are essential to develop a comfortable and tension-free audition performance. The two primary tools needed to construct a solid audition foundation are an expressive voice and a flexible body. No actor can afford the luxury of sloppy or slurred speech — sometimes referred to as "lazy lips" — or a lifeless body in an audition. The voice needs to be tuned and the body toned in regular rehearsal sessions to meet the vocal and physical demands of the text.

Additional Dimensions

Here are some additional audition principles to review in the rehearsal period as part of your audition preparation. A first principle is the need to maintain at least three copies of the audition monologue. The first copy is marked in colored pencil to chart preliminary character actions or intentions and to indicate the build to a climax. The second copy is marked in a different colored pencil to chart potential vocal or physical responses and also indicates subtle movement opportunities. This copy may also include a colored code of operative words or phrases that lend themselves to individual word play or meaningful gestures. The first two copies of the monologue should be used exclusively in the rehearsal period, allowing for refinement or revision as inventive new character insights surface. At the end of the rehearsal period, a well-designed audition blueprint should emerge in a third copy of the monologue. The third copy should be used to polish vocal and physical choices made for the audition performance.

A second principle is the need to understand the audition etiquette of introducing yourself and the monologue you are performing. Do not think of the introduction as a "non-performance" moment. It is, in fact, your first entrance on-stage and should be marked with poise and self-confidence. The spoken introduction is memorized and should be brief — thirty seconds is sufficient — and cordial. A typical audition introduction might simply say, "Hello. My name is_____. I'll be doing monologues from Wendy Wasserstein's *Uncommon Women* and Paula Vogel's *The Baltimore Waltz*." You may also choose to indicate the name of the monologue characters and the setting if time permits.

If you are performing two contrasting monologues in an audition, introduce both of them at the beginning and then use brief spoken transitions to move easily from one to the other. Of course, if you are performing only one monologue, then it is only necessary to use a brief introduction to set the scene. Transitions should also be memorized and include brief remarks that identify the monologue character, setting, and situation. Don't forget to pause before and after an introduction or a transition. A typical transition for a monologue from Athol Fugard's *My Children! My Africa!*, for example, might say, "Isabel, a disillusioned young woman damaged by a recent incident of racial violence in her homeland of South Africa, shares her troubled thoughts with a former high school friend."

A third principle is the need to anticipate a callback for final casting consideration. Although final audition materials — cold readings, duo scenes, or small group work — are usually chosen for an actor and distributed at callback, you should be prepared for an improvisation, directed reading, or another brief interview session with the director. Remember to arrive early for a callback, and don't forget to budget time for vocal and physical relaxation exercises before the scheduled appointment. Always be attentive to the callback order of scheduled actors. Know who you follow so that last-minute emergencies like a missing button, dry throat, or restroom pause will not distract your focus. It may be a good idea to wear the same audition wardrobe to callback in order to refresh the director's memory of the initial look that earned you another performance opportunity. Finally, it may also be useful to prepare an autobiographical mini-monologue for those auditions in which you may be asked to briefly describe yourself as part of an informal interview. Think of the mini-monologue — perhaps titled "The Me Nobody Knows" — as an expressive "self-portrait" that captures the enduring spirit of your inner self. Short anecdotes, comic mishaps, unusual hobbies, recent events, favorite books, or career goals are ripe material for a two or three minute glimpse of who you are as a person. The mini-monologue might also suggest what it would be like to work with you in a more formal rehearsal setting.

Although the primary source of performance materials is found in anthologies or play collections edited specifically for auditions or scene study, you should make use of the acting edition of a playscript if it is available. The acting edition is a chronicle of the final production of a text, and may include stage directions or other theatrical elements that helped frame the text as it emerged in rehearsal or in production. The acting edition may also provide additional character clues for interpretation, movement, or staging. Acting editions of a text are relatively inexpensive and may be purchased directly from catalogues of well-known publishers like Dramatists Play Service, Inc., Samuel French, Inc., Contemporary Drama Service, or the Theatre Communications Group. Please see the Supplemental Resource Materials at the end of the book for additional information on these and other valuable theatre resources.

Supplementary Audition Resources

One of the challenges for an actor is to continue to discover imaginative texts that have audition potential. Time and energy must be set aside for re-reading familiar texts, reviewing new texts, or searching for adapted materials from non-dramatic sources that may have a strong sense of theatricality in performance. There are a number of resources available to actors who may have limited experience in reading non-dramatic materials with an eye to adapting or editing them for a monologue audition. Song lyrics, film scripts, short stories, narrative poems, memoirs, and historical biographies and diaries frequently provide imaginative non-dramatic character portraits for auditions that do not require monologues from traditional theatre playscripts.

The primary challenge in playing non-dramatic materials is to identify unique character portraits and then to adapt a meaningful series of significant events or incidents that build moment-to-moment audience anticipation. However, in comparison to the now shopworn audition monologues of familiar authors, original adaptations from unfamiliar texts may offer exciting new character portraits that complement an actor's individual performance skills. Adapting non-dramatic materials for an audition involves careful editing to isolate memorable theatrical moments and timely transitions that punctuate the dramatic action described in the text. It is important that the adaptation (a) focus on a single character point of view, (b) feature a significant conflict, (c) build to a memorable climax, and (d) promote vocal and physical opportunities for performance. Some examples of non-dramatic audition materials might include the dramatic narratives of Ntozake Shange, Anna Deavere Smith's character sketches in *Fire in the Mirror*, Eudora Welty's short story "Why I Live at the P.O." or the collected essays of the novelist and poet Joyce Carol Oates.

Regular reading of new texts or attending theatre performances — especially staged readings or studio productions of new or experimental plays — may also help identify potential monologues that are fresh in both character types and roles. Supplementary sources, however, should suit the specific audition call and provide a three-dimensional range of character development if they are to be competitive with more traditional texts. The final choices you make should clearly establish your age, vocal range, and physical type. Just remember that whatever is *descriptive* in non-dramatic literature must become *active* in an audition performance.

Sample Rehearsal Readings

The following sample rehearsal readings are original texts, not excerpts of longer character speeches from traditional full-length playscripts. They are independent theatrical episodes or character monologues written to initially challenge you in classroom discussion and performance. The samples do, however, share many of the same life experiences and points of view that you would expect to find in longer texts. Each sample presents well-developed and distinctive character portraits that should stimulate your creative talents. You should use these rehearsal materials to design an initial audition blueprint most appropriate to your understanding of the basic practices discussed in Chapter 1.

Begin with a close reading of each monologue to identify those that best suit your age range, vocal quality, or physical type. Then determine which of the samples are most compatible with your own personal views on the issues being addressed. Your initial review should also provide a glimpse of the "self-image" for each character — especially in terms of age, height, weight, and posture. With these preliminary views in mind, give some thought to each character's action, attitude, and intention in the monologues that you would like to explore in more detail.

Using character clues indicated in the brief introduction to each sample reading, make specific performance choices and identify a clear set of character objectives that you will pursue. Then determine what role, if any, hand props, wardrobe, and movement might play for each of the characters you will perform. When you have made these initial decisions — based upon several readings of your individual choices — give some thought to staging each sample. Finally, work on a brief, spoken introduction for each of your monologue choices. The self-confidence and experience you gain in translating these basic performance practices into a personal audition blueprint will be useful in Chapter 2, when the focus shifts to polishing skills in analysis and rehearsal techniques.

Blind Dog
by Tom Coash

1   *Beth, a young woman trapped in a nightmare marriage to an*
2   *abusive and cold-hearted husband, struggles to free herself*
3   *from a life of brutality. Teetering on the brink of a collapsing*
4   *marriage, painful images of a childhood incident with a blind*
5   *dog emerge, and Beth struggles to come to terms with the*
6   *conflicting emotional memories of the dog and her own*
7   *thoughts of self-destruction.*
8

9   BETH: I always did what I was told. That's the way it
10   was in our house. My father would say, "A man's home
11   is his castle." My mother would say, "Obey your father."
12   Bobby was like that song "Misguided Angel." This
13   misunderstood, misguided angel. My parents hated him.
14   We ran away, got married, came home, and right away
15   Bobby started in on his improving-Beth program. I had
16   to be just so, the meals just so. Didn't like my friends,
17   didn't like my parents, didn't like my hair, didn't like my
18   attitude. And I obeyed. Honor and obey, right? I was
19   focusing so hard on making sure that everything was
20   perfect that I didn't have room to think of anything else.
21   Have his socks washed. Have dinner on the table at
22   exactly five-thirty p.m. Of course, he didn't always come
23   home at five-thirty p.m., so I'd just sit by the stove and
24   wait. I'm serious. Anything to avoid a fight. My mother
25   said, "Good husbands are made by God, good marriages
26   by women." My father said, "You made your own bed,
27   now lie in it."
28   So, Valentine's Day, I wanted to make him happy,
29   do it right, you know? I copied this recipe out of about

1   a ninety dollar cookbook at the Barnes and Noble, prime
2   rib stuffed with lobster. It was the fanciest thing I ever
3   made, took me all day. And ... he never came home. I left
4   it sitting there on the table with all the hearts and candles.
5   Two a.m. he comes in, drunk, looks at the meat sitting
6   there all congealed and says, "What is this? How much
7   money did you waste on this crap?" I started yelling at him
8   and he hit me in the mouth. I never imagined anything like
9   that, you know? I couldn't believe that he was actually
10   hitting me, that it was actually happening.
11   One time when I was a kid, we were all out playing in
12   the park and this old blind dog came up to us. Its eyes
13   were all glazed over and milky, just running around lost.
14   But it was real friendly and you could see it belonged to
15   somebody 'cause it had a collar. You'd call it and it'd wag
16   its tail like crazy and come running to your voice all
17   trusting. Trusted you. Then these older kids came along
18   and started calling the dog — only they'd stand behind a
19   fence or a tree and the dog would come running and run
20   straight into the tree, hard. And they kept doing it over
21   and over and laughing, and the dog kept coming to the
22   voice and wham into another tree, wham, into the slide,
23   wham ... Finally the dog just stood there, shivering, afraid
24   to move. I ran home crying and told my mother, and my
25   father came in and I told him and then he went out and
26   shot that dog. Shot it. Said it was the kindest thing.
27   You ever feel like that dog? People call you, you jump
28   up, wag your tail, and wham, run head first into a big old
29   tree. Wham ... wham. I do. Sometimes I feel just like that
30   dog.

Kelly
by Shirley King

1   *Kelly, a feisty and unflappable flight attendant, is on a*
2   *hilarious first-class journey of career burn-out, and the trip is*
3   *a lively and amusing aerial assault on her unsuspecting*
4   *passengers. Fasten your seat belt! This non-stop laugh express*
5   *should have them running for the emergency exits and*
6   *wondering if Kelly has already logged far too many air miles!*
7

8   KELLY: Ladies and gentlemen, welcome. This is Kelly,
9   your flight attendant, speaking. Please take your seats
10   and fasten your seat belts. Put your seats in the upright
11   position. Raise your tables and secure the latches.
12   When the cabin sign goes off, if it ever does, you may
13   move about the aircraft. But not until then. Smoking is
14   prohibited. No smoking in seats and none in the
15   lavatories. None whatever. This is punishable by a
16   humongous fine and serious jail time.
17   Question about boarding? Oh, very well. Chaotic?
18   Well, why wouldn't it be? Not our fault. First we tried
19   boarding by rows. Well, you know how that went. You
20   people shove, you bellow, you stampede, ignoring all
21   decorum. Next, whimsical boarding, based on hair color,
22   shoe size, and team logo tee shirts. But arguments
23   ensued. Should Atlanta Braves fans board before
24   Arizona Diamondbacks? Yes, alphabetically speaking,
25   Arizona does come before Atlanta. On the other hand,
26   Atlanta is merely a city while Arizona is a state. Surely
27   you see the dilemma. So we tried random boarding. You
28   larger, quicker passengers are free to seize the best
29   seats, and if you trample each other, not our problem.

1   Understood? Good. No more questions now. We are
2   preparing for takeoff.
3   Turn off your cellular phones, computers, pagers, and
4   listening devices. Do not beg for food. We no longer serve
5   food. You should have made provisions earlier. Actually,
6   we still do serve drinks. Ten dollars for mixed drinks, five
7   for sodas and juices. You are allowed only one drink per
8   flight. If you request another you will be wrestled to the
9   cabin floor and arrested. Remember, ladies and
10   gentlemen, you have been warned.
11   Questions are now allowed. They may or may not be
12   answered. "If you become a flight attendant what are your
13   duties?" Thank you for asking. You will schlep drinks
14   across several time zones, confiscate personal
15   possessions, deal with rowdy passengers — question? The
16   upside? That is the upside. Oh, did I forget to mention
17   Scramble Time? Every thirty minutes you will all change
18   seats. This prevents circulatory problems while providing
19   an opportunity to meet people you would otherwise shun.
20   Before landing, you should know all about each other's
21   family problems, height, weight, and bank balances. This
22   is important information. Use it wisely.
23   All right, ladies and gentlemen, the cabin sign is off.
24   Grab those carry-a-boards and step lively. People? What
25   are you waiting for? Go, go, go! Scramble!

Paranoid
by Deborah Maddox

1   *In this brief, searing episode, a mentally fragile teenager has*
2   *been diagnosed as "paranoid" and is confined to a hospital.*
3   *Although she is under the close supervision of a psychiatric*
4   *doctor, the young girl is so traumatized with fear that she*
5   *cannot determine the difference between illusion and*
6   *reality — and she is being catapulted swiftly toward*
7   *madness. Here she cries out for relief from the haunting terror*
8   *that is crippling her life.*
9
10   TEENAGER: You have to be smart and look around the
11   corners! Always look around the corners. And don't
12   forget to check underneath the bed. Why? Because ...
13   they always hide in those places. And their voices. Oh,
14   God ... all of those voices, crying out. Can't you hear
15   them? Listen! Listen to them! Sleep? I don't want to
16   sleep! If I sleep, they will get me. Why can't you
17   understand that? I keep telling you. If I sleep, they will
18   get me. Please don't let them get me. Just tell them to
19   shut up and go away. I can't take it anymore! The
20   voices ... the screaming ... the yelling ... they are so
21   loud. And the laughing. Why are they laughing? Please
22   help me. Just make them go away. No ... don't leave me
23   alone in this room another night! No! Don't go! I'll be
24   good. I promise. Please, Doctor, I promise to be good.
25   Don't let them get me! No, don't leave!

Alone in the Crowd
by Gail Blanton

1   *This dark re-telling of biblical passages Mark 5:24-33 and*
2   *Philippians 2:1-4 features an unidentified woman who sits*
3   *quietly alone during a Sunday worship service. In silence,*
4   *she re-examines the meaning of life and her commitment to*
5   *the church. Feeling isolated and unloved, even after twelve*
6   *years of devotion to the same church, she faces the*
7   *bittersweet reality of still feeling "alone in the crowd" and*
8   *unable to move on with life.*
9
10 WOMAN: Here I am, back in church again this week,
11 and I'm supposed to be all joyful and excited, part of
12 God's big, happy family. Supposed to be living a
13 meaningful life, fulfilled in my career, enjoying close
14 relationships with many different people. But here's how
15 it really is. If I were to die tomorrow, nobody would even
16 know it. Oh, I mean, they'd know it, but it's not like
17 anybody would care. Seven years I've been at my job. A
18 thousand people there, I guess, but it's like one big
19 Xerox machine. Punch my ID card in the lock and here
20 come the photocopies: "Good morning," "Good
21 morning," "Good morning," "Have a nice day," "Have a
22 nice day," "Have a nice day." I don't need a nice day. I
23 need somebody to say, "Hey, you did a great job." I'd
24 like somebody to listen to my opinion. I'd like somebody
25 to think I'm worth a raise. I'd like somebody to
26 remember my name. It's not like it's much better at
27 church. Twelve years I've been here, but it seems like
28 I'm always just on the fringe of belonging. I've visited
29 this group or that, but I just don't seem to fit anywhere.

1   I'm here most every Sunday, give offerings, always bring
2   something for the mission project boxes and dessert for
3   fellowships. I've tried to set up lunches or shopping with
4   several people — even offered to baby sit, but nobody ever
5   follows through. To tell the truth, I don't know what the
6   problem is. I've tried everything I know. Always in this big
7   crowd, but I'm so lonely I could die. I wish I had just one
8   real friend. But it's just "Praise the Lord," "Praise the
9   Lord," "Praise the Lord." "Praying for you," "Praying for
10 you," "Praying for you" — photocopies again. They just
11 keep on shooting out of that big, impersonal motor.
12 Sometimes I'd like to reach out and pry open that machine
13 and see what's really inside. But it's hard to put your hand
14 where you know it's going to be burned.

Walking Sideways
by Ruth McKee

1　*This somber excerpt from "Walking Sideways," reveals Carol,*
2　*a mature woman and stay-at-home mother, sitting silently in*
3　*a brightly-lit public school classroom as she listens to the*
4　*teacher behind the desk. Twisting uneasily in a child's chair*
5　*that's much too small, Carol grows increasingly anxious and*
6　*is unable to grasp the painful truth that her son — who*
7　*brought a steak knife to school and then threatened other*
8　*students — may need to attend a special school.*
9
10　**CAROL: Jimmy's always been difficult. Different.**
11　**Special. Ever since he learned to crawl — didn't want to**
12　**move straightforward, always trying to sidestep, so his**
13　**eyes could always be out, looking around. I should really**
14　**get those eyes checked, though. Maybe there's been**
15　**something wrong with them from the beginning. He**
16　**didn't want to move right out in front because he might**
17　**bump into something.**
18　**And now he can't see the blackboard, I bet. So you**
19　**just put him up in the front row where he can see and**
20　**I'm sure he'll stop fidgeting. And I'll get his eyes**
21　**checked, we'll get those glasses. It happens to a lot of**
22　**kids. How can you expect a kid to learn when they can't**
23　**see the blackboard? So they start to fall behind.**
24　**I know that you can't worry about every single one**
25　**of them when you have thirty-three. I'm sure sometimes**
26　**all of them get out of hand. They have their bad days.**
27　**All of us do, right?** *(She laughs.)*
28　**But he's a good kid, really.**
29　**His father's away in the service. Infantry. He's in Iraq**

1   right now. So I'm sure Jimmy — it's a game he likes to
2   play. Defending his country. It's just a game he plays with
3   his friends — they play for hours in the backyard, shooting
4   each other and falling down, you know like little boys like
5   to do? His father took him to paintball when he was back
6   for his sixteen days, and ever since then ...
7   Jimmy doesn't actually want to kill people. He doesn't
8   want to hurt people. He wouldn't hurt a ... Little boys fight.
9   It's his father's job for godsakes, he's just learning. The
10   skills. You need. To live.
11   Maybe your life is all wine and roses, but it's not like
12   that for the rest of us. I've got two other kids; I can't be
13   watching him all the time. But I would know if my son was
14   up to no good. I would hear about it, wouldn't I? He's not
15   like other kids. He's shy. He's never been a very good
16   student, and that hurts. Especially when ... especially
17   when he's in a class like here. And you know. *(She gets*
18   *intimate, then retreats.)*
19   Well, he speaks English at home. So you think he'd be
20   a better student at least than some of them. So it's hard
21   on the kid. We've moved four times, each new school is a
22   new challenge. And here ...
23   Those kids pick on him. I don't know how much of it
24   you've seen, how much happens in the classroom, but it's
25   they, who ... You can see how he'd want to protect himself,
26   can't you? I'd want to protect myself if I were in his place.
27   His daddy ... A steak knife is not a weapon, it's a kitchen
28   tool. My son doesn't need a special school.
29   Everything will be fine when I get him those glasses.

All James
by Leigh Podgorski

1   *Tykira, a brash, street-wise teenage girl, has been arrested*
2   *and is being held in a jail cell as a co-defendant in the recent*
3   *brutal murder of an elderly lady. She is speaking to her*
4   *attorney, describing the grisly incident in graphic detail and*
5   *placing the blame on her boyfriend, James. Tykira's chilling*
6   *story, however, concludes with a surprising confession that*
7   *reveals the sober reality of her disturbing relationship with*
8   *James.*
9
10   TYKIRA: Look, don't get mad or nothin', OK? But I
11   think the way you're doin' this thing ain't the best way
12   it should be done. I can see the judge, I mean, I'm
13   sittin' right there, an' I can see him gettin' annoyed
14   when you keep askin' all those questions over and over
15   again with these witnesses. Jus' ask 'em a few
16   questions an' sit down. It'll be better that way. Look, I
17   don't want nobody feelin' sorry for me, OK? — or feelin'
18   they got to take some kind of mercy on me. I jus' wish
19   I could get somebody to understand me, to understand
20   where I'm comin' from, but no one can seem to do that.
21   I'm sorry she's dead — but I didn't have nothin' to do
22   with her bein' dead. You understand? I tried to steal the
23   car. OK. I can cop to that. I wanted her car, an' I was
24   in on takin' it after we dumped her body in that vacant
25   lot, but that's all I was in on. The rest of it, that was all
26   James. It was James who got her to take us for a ride
27   in that car. James who made sure I was in the front seat
28   so's I could drop my cell phone an' distract her. James
29   who lunged forward from the back seat an' wrapped that

1 telephone cord 'round her neck. James. All James.
2 The only reason I cut her was I was tryin' to cut the cord
3 from off her neck. I had that steak knife, an' there she was
4 gaggin' an' fightin' for breath, an' I took the knife out an'
5 tried to save her life. An' I was scared to death the whole
6 time I was doin' it. You've seen James. You know how he
7 is. I was scared to death he was goin' to kill me next, an'
8 that's the truth of the matter. Nobody should go to prison
9 for the rest of their life 'cause they tried to steal a car.
10 Nobody, especially not a kid. *(Beat.)*
11   I heard that judge say James is takin' the stand this
12 afternoon. Is that right? That's funny. I don't know how
13 long it's been since I seen him. As long as I've been in
14 here, which is like forever now. He wrote me at first, but
15 that's stopped now. I heard he was sleepin' with
16 somebody. Imagine that. How he gonna work out a thing
17 like that in here? Look, you gotta question him, right? So
18 I was thinkin' of some good things to ask him, an' this is
19 what I thought. *(She pulls a paper from her pocket.)* That one
20 there — that'd be the best one to start off with. "James,
21 do you still love Tykira?" *(Beat.)*
22   I think so. I think that'd be the best way to go.

How Could You?
by Samara Siskind

1   *Priscilla, an adolescent young girl drowning in the rough seas*
2   *of teenage angst, is enraged to the point of murderous intent*
3   *after hearing a vicious rumor about her romantic feelings*
4   *being broadcast publicly by her best friend, Emily. In a comic*
5   *war of words, Priscilla confronts her best friend and is so*
6   *ecstatic to learn the "other side" of the rumor that she and*
7   *Emily reconcile and celebrate their friendship with a warm*
8   *embrace.*
9

10   **PRISCILLA: You did not! You did not! I can't believe you**
11   **Emily! I thought we were friends? Best friends! How**
12   **could you do this to me? I have been like, the bestest**
13   **friend to you! Who brought you your homework for three**
14   **weeks when you got mono from Justin Fromeyer, huh?**
15   **Who was the only person who didn't laugh and call you**
16   **"Bride of Jaws" when your parents refused to get you**
17   **invisible braces? Who held your hand when you got your**
18   **nose pierced? Who tells you that you look cute in jeans**
19   **that are totally like, two sizes too small? Me, that's who,**
20   **and this ...** *this* **is how you repay me?**
21   **Honestly, I don't think I'll ever be able to forgive you,**
22   **Emily.** *(Beat.)* **For what? Oh, come on.** *(Scathing)* **You**
23   **know what you did ...** *(Takes a deep breath.)* **You told Zach**
24   **I** *liked* **him. Jackie Prince's sister's friend's cousin told**
25   **Melanie's little brother's girlfriend, who told Bethany,**
26   **who told me after third period. Apparently Jackie**
27   **Prince's sister's friend's cousin saw you and Zach**
28   **standing by his locker talking and whispering together.**
29   **So there. Your web of betrayal has been unraveled, and**

1   now it's all out in the open. So Emily ... What do you have
2   to say for yourself? *(Beat.)*
3   What? You're kidding me. Zach likes me too? *(Jumps*
4   *around in celebration.)* Oh, dear Emily! Why didn't you say
5   so in the first place? How do I look? How do I smell? Where
6   is he? Do I look hot? *(Beat. She stops jumping.)* Wait a sec,
7   Emily, I'm going to ask you a question ... and it's like
8   totally the most important thing I'm ever going to ask you.
9   It's like, my whole life depends on it. OK, ready? Listen
10 very closely. Does Zach like me ... or does he ... or does
11 he *like me* like me?

These Are Real
by Louise Rozett

1   *In* These Are Real, *a venomous actress deftly turns her*
2   *acceptance speech at the Academy Awards ceremony into a*
3   *blistering and terribly funny tirade directed at those who*
4   *tormented her as a teenager. Offering a crisply-wrapped*
5   *package of resentment with deep undertones of diabolical*
6   *delight, the actress embraces one hilarious acknowledgment*
7   *after another until she takes a final, triumphant curtain call.*
8

9   **ACTRESS:** *(Enters with statuette and index card.)* **Ladies**
10   **and gentlemen, I — God, this is incredible!** *(Reading off*
11   *card)* **I cannot thank you enough for this! It is such an**
12   **honor to be recognized by the Academy! There are so**
13   **many people to thank, so many. Of course, my**
14   **wonderful parents and husband and sons, and my**
15   **director and fellow actors, and all the people who had**
16   **the faith in me to keep sending me back to rehab.**
17   *(She looks up from her card to the audience.)* **But,**
18   **actually — you know what? There are a few individuals**
19   **who really deserve this statuette more than I do, and I'd**
20   **like to personally recognize them.** *(She throws the card*
21   *over her shoulder.)* **I'd like to thank all those boys out**
22   **there who never realized just how special I am, and who**
23   **told me no one would ever marry me. And, of course,**
24   **the girls in high school gym class who called me "hairy**
25   **hiney" when I came out of the shower or "big butt" when**
26   **I couldn't finish an aerobics class. If it weren't for all of**
27   **you, I never would have pushed myself as hard as I did**
28   **to get to this point, just so I could stand at this podium**
29   **and show you exactly what you missed out on. Let's**

1   take a moment to evaluate, shall we? What are you doing
2   with your lives? What are you doing ... right now?
3   Hmmmm? You're watching me, on screen, in front of the
4   entire world, and you are praying, praying that I'll say
5   "thanks" to our home town, or mention our high school.
6   Because you want people to know that I know you. Well,
7   here's a sweet little news flash. I don't even remember
8   your names. I wouldn't know you if I hit you with my limo.
9   Who's laughing now, baby? Huh?
10   *(She holds up the statuette, victory-style.)* Who's got the
11   pretty golden statuette? Who's the big movie star? *Me!* It's
12   *me!*
13   *(She taunts and threatens with it.)* And my life is great!
14   It's as great as it looks like it is!
15   *(She regains her composure.)* And I have you to thank for
16   that. All your insults and cruelties, all the times you stood
17   me up or ditched me, all the ways you tried to make
18   yourselves feel more important by hurting me. I wouldn't
19   trade a minute of that for all the Academy Awards in the
20   world. Because you, in your petty smallness, helped make
21   me who I am today. And I ... love ... me. Finally. And
22   these ... are real. Thank you.

Cookies
by Kathy Coudle King

1   *In* Cookies, *Shelia is a gutsy teen dressed in a Girl Scout*
2   *uniform and holding a clipboard. She stands center stage*
3   *with her hand raised as if she were about to knock on*
4   *someone's front door. Going door-to-door selling Girl Scout*
5   *cookies, Shelia gives new meaning to the phrase "Girl*
6   *Power!" Her self-confidence and poise also pay hefty*
7   *dividends when she shares her tips on how to succeed in*
8   *business ... without really trying.*
9

10   SHELIA: Beauty? Where did I learn about beauty?
11   Where does every girl learn? From magazines, of course.
12   My big sister has piles of them in her bedroom. She
13   hates for me to mess with her stuff, but whenever she's
14   not around, I sneak into her room. I'd take out the neat
15   pile she keeps by her bed. Carefully, so she wouldn't
16   even know I'd touch them, I'd flip the shiny pages,
17   breathe in the perfume scent, staring at all the faces of
18   the models, memorizing the way they smiled, or didn't,
19   the way they pouted, the way they leaned casually
20   against a car — or a guy. I studied the way they wore
21   their makeup, the colors of their lipstick, and their
22   hairstyles. I studied them and I learned. Wanna know
23   what I learned? *(Pause.)* I learned they all look alike!
24   They have the same shaped noses, eyes. Even the
25   shapes of their heads are the same. They're all the same
26   height, the same weight. Just like Barbie dolls, where
27   they say it's Latina Barbie on the box, but it's really just
28   white Barbie dipped in a tanning color with brown eyes
29   and hair. They change the wigs, duh. That's like the

1   girls in the magazines. They're all the same. After awhile,
2   I couldn't tell which magazines I'd looked at and which
3   ones I hadn't. See, they give you this recipe for how to be
4   beautiful. Buy this, wear your hair this way, dress that
5   way — but the recipe is like the kind you use with cookie
6   cutters, so every cookie comes out exactly the same.
7   No — *(Looking for word)* — variety. No surprises. That's
8   what I learned from beauty magazines. And me? I'm
9   nobody's cookie. Not your cupcake, not your honey, not
10   your little pumpkin, sweetie pie. I'm no cookie. But I'll sell
11   you some. How many cases do you want to buy?

Femonologues
by Jill Morley

1 *Maxine, an attractive and whimsical young woman bubbling*
2 *with theatrical vitality and a zest for the sentimental in life, is*
3 *an aspiring actress from Texas now working in a New York*
4 *City department store selling "Climax" perfume. There is a*
5 *surface glamour and shimmer about her that attracts a tidal*
6 *wave of admiring male customers to her sales counter. But*
7 *Maxine will have none of it and plays the game as effortlessly*
8 *as a chess master. Checkmate!*
9
10 MAXINE: "Climax!" Sample "Climax" today. Try the
11 only women's fragrance that builds to an evocative,
12 aromatic explosion. "Climax!" Are you looking for a gift
13 item, sir? Well, I'm afraid I cannot help you in that
14 department — just yet. I get off work at six p.m. Oh,
15 no, this is not my real job. I am really an actress. You
16 knew that? How? No, nothing you've probably seen, but
17 I'm in this wonderful class with a really good friend of a
18 friend of one of Lee Strasberg's former students who's
19 wonderful! *(To a prospective customer)* "Climax!" *(Back to*
20 *man)* I have done some of my best work in his class. I
21 have this one monologue that I do that is so good, tears
22 come to my eyes and everything. I am so sensitive. My
23 teacher says I am the female James Dean for the
24 millennium. And that's just how I come across on film!
25 On-stage, well, on-stage, I'm a regular Mary Louise
26 Jessica Parker! That was a joke that I made! Myself! I
27 like doing comedy, but with meaning. Like *Pretty*
28 *Woman.* I mean, that was art! The message! That once
29 you accept your station in life, you'll be swept off your

1   feet by an older man with money who'll take you shopping
2   at Chanel! The sentiment ... it's just so beautiful ... *(She*
3   *starts to cry.)* Oh here I go ... I am so sensitive. Oh, that
4   was truly a woman's film. Sorry for being so emotional. It's
5   just that for some reason, I feel close to you, like ... Sir,
6   is that a ring on your finger? It is, isn't it? Wife out of town
7   this weekend? Thought you'd do some local shopping,
8   hmmmm? Lunch? I don't do lunch with married men. Sir,
9   do you realize the stack of business cards I have in my
10   pockets? From men just like you who want ... a free
11   sample! Oh, my god! My manager is standing right next to
12   the Epilady counter. Buy something from me. *Now! (She*
13   *rings up the purchase, eyeing her manager.)* Here you go, sir.
14   I hope you enjoy your "Climax."

Chapter 2
Through the Looking Glass: Analysis and Rehearsal Techniques

"To hold, as 'twere, the mirror up to nature;
to show virtue her own feature, scorn her own image,
and the very age and body of the time his form and pressure."
— William Shakespeare, *Hamlet*

In his "advice to the players," Hamlet encourages the actor to be observant to everyday events and attentive to human nature in order to persuade the audience that what is seen and heard is both familiar and natural. This ability to create the illusion of reality in performance is also an essential ingredient in playscript analysis. One of the important roles that analysis plays in a monologue performance is to encourage a sense of **dramatic visualization**. Dramatic visualization is that uncanny ability to "see" believable characters in your mind's eye based solely on the written words or suggested actions in a printed text, and then to mirror that reflection in performance.

Text analysis is an orderly system of character interpretation and scene study techniques that should enhance your ability to accurately define a character in performance. Its basic practices provide the tools needed to design a compelling audition blueprint based on a disciplined study of the text rather than relying solely upon spontaneous impulse to sketch a character portrait. A carefully prepared analysis reveals what the character is feeling or thinking in a monologue, and may even suggest personal traits or behavior patterns to explore later in the rehearsal period. The most valuable role of text analysis, however, is that it teaches you how to decipher character actions or attitudes in a text and then translate them into a three-dimensional audition performance. That is why it is so important to read the *complete* playscript before turning your attention to the analysis of an individual monologue.

There are, of course, a number of theories on how to approach the study of a text with an eye to performance. The basic practices that follow are presented simply as guidelines to encourage you to make intellectual as well as emotional performance choices. There are no analysis laws or text formulas here, just a number of selected approaches to consider in the initial stages of playscript interpretation. The pursuit of a more individual style of text analysis will come later, when you are asked to design your own personal blueprint based on the practices you will learn in this chapter.

Basic Practices

Text analysis closely resembles the literary techniques used in a literature classroom to discover the complexities of character, plot, structure, and theme. Although it may be difficult for you to imagine yourself in a literature classroom intently studying a monologue before an audition, text analysis cannot be clearly understood without exploring its basic principles. First, take notes on the mental, physical, and vocal qualities of a character. Second, make initial decisions regarding the goals and objectives of a character. Third, define a character in terms of the author's explicit description. Fourth, visualize a character in terms of potential theatrical accessories like subtle wardrobe, hand props, stage business, or movement. Fifth, voice the attitude or mood of a character in tones suggested by the author's explicit words.

At first you may need to read the monologue silently, with an ear tuned to character interpretation and an eye focused on performance clues. The first reading should indicate the character's emotional or intellectual condition and whether or not you have the immediate personal identification needed to perform the character. A second reading should focus on *meaning* in terms of the character's word choice and point of view that may suggest movement or staging to help visualize the character in performance. The third reading should be a more spontaneous "performance" reading, voiced aloud to identify specific clues for character action, attitude, and intention.

These three basic steps of reading a text should help you more easily define who the character is, what the character is doing, where the character is doing it, when the character is doing it, and why the character is doing it. This invaluable information provides an accurate portrait of your character's action in the given circumstances of the text and may suggest a rough performance draft to pursue later in the rehearsal period. Frequent re-reading of the text should also reveal the four types of implicit or explicit action that you might choose to play in an audition. The four types are listed below for easy reference, and you should consider each of them in a preliminary approach to text analysis that leads to performance.

- **Character Action:** Individual habits, mannerisms, or personal traits of the character that surface from an analysis of the text.

- **Instinctive Action:** Spontaneous reactions or responses of the actor that surface in rehearsal as a result of individual habits, mannerisms, or personal traits of the character described in the text.

- **Descriptive Action:** Voice, gesture, and movement of the character that surfaces from an analysis of the dialogue and narrative description of the text.

- **Dramatic Action:** Conflict or complication needed to propel the character into incidents and events described in the text.

In making initial choices of character actions you wish to explore, a good starting point is to determine the most appropriate **mental symbol** that describes the character. A mental symbol indicates the overarching intention or motivation of a character, suggests what actions the character is willing to commit in order to achieve a specific goal, and underscores the price the character must pay to achieve that specific desire. For example, in Aristophanes' classical Greek comedy *Lysistrata*, the title character wishes to end the destructive Peloponnesian War that has been raging between Athens and Sparta. She is willing to defy tradition and rouse the women of Greece to engage in a "sex strike" until the men agree to sue for peace. The price she must pay for this act of comic defiance is the threat of verbal abuse, physical harm, and retribution.

Analysis Blueprint

A critical reading of a playscript should alert you to performance clues that may be suggested by the words or images in the text. There are some very common terms to consider in the design of an analysis blueprint. Being familiar with these terms should enable you to gain a deeper understanding of performance clues and how to identify them. Look for the **persona**, or "second self," of the author through whom the story is being told to identify the point of view. Examine the **storyline**, or sequence of events and incidents, to determine how place and time influence a character's action. Pay particular attention to the **denotative**, or "dictionary," meaning and the **connotative**, or "implied," meaning of the character's words to better understand the **subtext**, or hidden implication of the character's language. Identify the **climax**, or highest point in the dramatic action, and anticipate a similar build of intensity in a performance of the text.

Read the text as you might read a short biography or a novel, sorting out the characters and allowing the story to tell itself in the action, dialogue, and narrative. Don't forget to review the introduction to the text for any critical comments that may provide additional clues on character interpretation or author theme. The title of the text may suggest the author's point of view or indicate the theme as well. A character's name may even indicate a basic approach to understanding that character's action or intention in the text. Being aware of all these additional ingredients of analysis should amplify and reinforce your character interpretation and later performance. It also makes sense to pay careful attention to unfamiliar words, foreign terms, or subtle references to other literature or literary figures that might be casually mentioned in the text.

Some actors use their analysis blueprint to isolate and identify significant images, figurative language, or symbols that give added dimension in voicing a character's dialogue. Other actors use a dictionary to paraphrase their analysis blueprint into conversational words and phrases. Others reduce a character's thoughts, actions, and ideas to one-word nouns or verbs that can be explored later in the rehearsal period. Still other actors use a **performance metaphor** — an implied analogy or comparison which imaginatively identifies the character with something else discovered in analysis — to help visualize a character's attitude, mood, or intention in the text.

As your own individual style of text analysis emerges, you will discover that the actor's eye can be trained to respond creatively to theatrical images that are inherent or implied in a playscript. Understanding the basic ingredients of analysis will give you the critical skills necessary to read and interpret a text with keen insight. The more knowledge you acquire about the text, the more perceptive will be your interpretation of the character and the action in the text. That is why this approach to analysis requires a flexible and responsive reading style to capture and catalogue the flurry of vivid images — spoken and unspoken — that need to be translated from the page to the stage.

Rehearsal Techniques

The rehearsal period is a pre-performance laboratory where you begin to experiment with an analysis blueprint and refine character interpretation. It provides a risk-free space in which to discover the vocal and physical qualities that best convey your character's action, attitude, and intention. The rehearsal period is an opportunity for you to fill in any blanks left unanswered in the analysis blueprint, particularly if you have not been able to connect the dots of your character's action and intention. The rehearsal period is a time to call upon your "memory book" of life experiences that may provide complementary gestures or mannerisms to use as a subtle nuance to enhance the character portrait. The rehearsal period is also a final opportunity to discover if a monologue has sufficient implicit or explicit theatricality to meet audition performance guidelines.

Regardless of the approach you take in the rehearsal period, there are a number of expectations that should be met to give purpose and rigor to an audition performance. The rehearsal period should have a regular schedule of time devoted to (a) interpretation of text, (b) vocal and physical exercises, (c) movement, and (d) performance of text. The time devoted to interpretation should divide the monologue into a series of character intentions or objectives called **beats**. A beat begins when a character's intention begins and ends with its completion. Identifying the sequence of beats will give a sense of tempo or rhythm to your performance. The interpretation segment of the rehearsal period might also include exploring an **inner monologue**, or what the actor is thinking as the character is speaking. The inner monologue is similar to the subtext, which was mentioned earlier in the discussion, and can be used to highlight a character's primary intention or objective in a monologue.

The time devoted to vocal and physical exercises should include an alternating schedule of relaxation and warm-up exercises. A rehearsal routine that regularly tunes the voice and tones the body should condition you to respond efficiently and promptly to any vocal or physical demand of the text. A rehearsal routine that includes relaxation and warm-up exercises also helps to effectively combat initial stage fright associated with performance. The time devoted to movement should explore the role of the body as a fluid, expressive, and relaxed instrument that conveys a visual portrait of the monologue character. A movement rehearsal should include staging the text and focusing on subtle character bodily actions or gestures that are compatible with the character portrait. The time to refine and polish the performance should be determined after character interpretation, vocal and physical qualities, movement, and staging are firmly set. Remember that the rehearsal time reserved to refine and polish will also need to include memorizing text, writing an introduction and any essential transitions, and practicing the skillful use of accessories like hand props and any other stage business that may be part of the performance.

Additional Dimensions

For most actors, stage fright is not difficult to describe. For some actors, however, it is difficult to control. Actors frequently refer to "going up" when anxiety or apprehension — key words in defining stage fright — cause them to forget lines, miss cues, mix up stage business, or confuse movement directions during an audition or a performance. Try not to be overly concerned about performance anxiety or apprehension. You should be prepared through a focused routine of analysis and rehearsal to improvise or paraphrase a monologue in any unexpected circumstance. Learn to go on as if any hesitation or momentary lapse were just a thoughtful character pause that is part of the performance. You can reduce the possibility of mishaps in an audition or a performance through an additional series of regular rehearsals that focus on good memorization skills, line readings, or repetition exercises. Remember to always practice dialogue *aloud* in rehearsal periods set aside to polish text interpretation or to memorize character lines.

Breathing Machine

It is important in the rehearsal period to explore proper breathing and vocal relaxation techniques that produce meaningful sounds without strain or tension on your "breathing machine." Diaphragmatic breathing provides the greatest lung expansion and is the least likely to cause tension in the vocal muscles. It also provides the necessary rhythmic air pressure needed to voice sounds with the least strain or exertion. Begin by lying flat on your back and relaxing completely. Place your hand just above your waistline and begin to breathe slowly and deeply. As you breathe, pay attention to the expansion and contraction of the diaphragm, and notice how the abdominal wall moves in and out as your breathing is consciously directed and controlled.

After several minutes, or when you understand how proper diaphragmatic breathing feels, stand up and repeat the exercise. Keep your hand at your waist to detect any change in the center of breathing and voice aloud some selected lines from your monologue. If your breathing appears to be centered in the upper chest and the abdominal wall is not actively in motion, practice slower and deeper breathing. Encourage your diaphragm to expand and contract with a comfortable rhythm, and concentrate on keeping the upper chest from rising and falling. Repeating this exercise several times at short intervals during the rehearsal period should result in better voice control and production. The exercise also lends itself to a vocal relaxation technique to practice before an audition performance.

Body Image

The role of the body in performance is just as important as proper breathing techniques. Consider, for example, that your voice and breathing technique will be greatly influenced by your body responses. A relaxed and comfortable posture will enhance breathing and result in fluent and expressive speech. To tone your "body image" in the rehearsal period, begin by holding your body erect with chest high, chin up, back flat, and arms and legs straight. Place one foot slightly in front of the other, with the weight centered on the ball of the forward foot. This position should create an alert visual portrait and facilitate movement to convey changing character attitudes or moods. Now spread your legs slightly so you have a solid sense of balance. Let your upper body sag so that your head and arms slowly dangle toward the floor, like a puppet on a string. Swing your arms forward and backward in a slow rhythm. Voice the sounds "ah" and "oh" in an intonation that parallels the movement of your body swaying to-and-fro. Now, slowly raise your body while continuing to swing your arms forward and backward in a slow rhythm. When you are standing upright, begin to rotate your head in a slow circle left to right and then right to left. Repeat the "ah" and "oh" sounds in short bursts, then slightly longer bursts, and then in the longest bursts possible on only one breath.

You should have experienced a marked release of anxiety and tension at the end of this brief physical relaxation exercise. If you do not feel relaxed, it may be necessary to repeat the exercise several times at a slower rate. When confident that your body image is sufficiently tuned, it is a good time to refine your character's bodily actions, gestures, and stage movement. This exercise also lends itself to a physical relaxation technique to practice before an audition performance.

Audition Style

The style of an audition is the "personal signature" you present to an audience. Style refers to the spark of energy and vitality that indicates an actor's stage personality. The actor is organized and well prepared. The introduction, movement, and staging is crisp. The audience "sees" and "hears" a polished vocal and physical expression of the actor's immediate identification with the character portrait being performed. There is a clear and focused attention on the character's attitude, action, and intention in the given circumstances of the text. The energy level is high, and there is an unmistakable sense that this is a complex character portrait being performed with depth and dimension.

Sample Rehearsal Readings

The following sample rehearsal readings are original texts, not excerpts of longer character speeches from traditional full-length playscripts. They are independent theatrical episodes or character monologues written specifically to cultivate analysis skills and to enhance rehearsal techniques. The samples do, however, offer a new flavor and texture of emotions and situations that lend themselves to an analysis approach that defines a character in terms of action, attitude, and intention. There are challenging performance opportunities here for the actor who wishes to explore serious character portraits that demand fresh and thoughtful performance approaches. There are also a number of comic portraits that feature colorful figures engaged in humorous situations. You should use these rehearsal materials to clarify your understanding of basic analysis practices and then design your own personal analysis blueprint based on the principles discussed in this chapter.

Begin, as you did in Chapter 1, with a close reading of each monologue to identify those that are most appropriate for your age range, vocal quality, or physical type. Give serious thought to the complex characters that appear to lend themselves to a detailed analysis blueprint. Then determine if the "inner life" — personal philosophy, point of view, and individual personality — of each character you have selected is compatible with your own views on the issues being addressed in the text. Now narrow your focus to determine which characters provide the best opportunity for you to play the role with conviction while at the same time displaying your vocal and physical skills.

For each character you would like to explore in the rehearsal period, write a one-page character sketch that briefly outlines the mental, physical, and vocal qualities of that figure. Begin to visualize each character in terms of theatrical accessories like subtle wardrobe, hand props, or stage business. As individual images begin to surface, give some thought to the four types of character actions described at the beginning of the chapter. Then choose one appropriate action for each character that you would like to explore in the rehearsal period. Make sure that you have good variety in your choices of action — character, instinctive, descriptive, or dramatic — and that your choices are based on the given circumstances described in the text. Finally, include a "mental symbol" for each character in your analysis blueprint, and then explore all of these choices in the rehearsal period.

The critical skills in analysis and rehearsal techniques that you cultivate here using original texts will be an invaluable asset in future audition preparation. Those skills will be especially useful to give life and meaning to the monologue and duologue characters from full-length texts that are included in the following chapters. As you continue on your journey to meet the interesting characters waiting for you, leave nothing to chance. Assume a performance attitude that is simple and subtle, and present your characters with clarity and precision.

Next

by Amy Berlin

1   *A free-spirited but frustrated actress strikes a pose center stage*
2   *and speaks directly to the audience. She exhibits an intoxicating*
3   *mix of mirth and mayhem as she recounts the trials and*
4   *tribulations of theatre auditions. This hilarious tirade on*
5   *thespian regrets and missed opportunities also teaches a playful*
6   *lesson to all who tread the boards: Alas, even when you think*
7   *you are perfect for a role, all you may hear is a lightning-fast,*
8   *"Next!"*
9
10 ACTRESS: So, it's been a bad month, audition-wise. I
11 mean, not to sound like every other actress in the world,
12 but I'm getting really tired. I'm tired of trying to impress
13 less-talented people than me; tired of trying to prove
14 something to people who wouldn't know talent if it bit
15 them on the toe. I'm just tired of trying and trying, just to
16 get a part ... that I would be amazing in. I mean, not to be
17 conceited — and I guess everyone says this — but they
18 would be *lucky* to have me. *Lucky.* But there's just no
19 vision.
20   They all want the same thing. Thin, small, blond,
21 pretty ... blah, blah, blah. Even when the part's supposed
22 to be "plain" or "homely." It's still the same thing: I show
23 up ... and, uh ... "Next!" I swear to you, if I wrote a play
24 based on me, described exactly as I am, I would probably
25 show up for the auditions and ... "Next!"
26   Actually, I really do have a great idea for a play. It's
27 been percolating below the surface while I go from audition
28 to audition. You know, the creativity's been bubbling while
29 I knock myself out trying to get a part as Maid Number

1 Three or Chorus Flower-Seller. Now, that's "true art,"
2 wouldn't you say? I mean, that's why I spent years in
3 school studying Stanislavski and Meisner — so I could
4 really be in the moment marching in when the lead yells,
5 "Guards, take them away!" And there I come, marching
6 bravely for my few seconds on-stage. All motivated and in
7 character and ... over in a heartbeat.
8   But I digress. My play. OK, it's about this thirty-five
9 year-old, tall, curly brown-haired, sarcastic Jewish girl. So,
10 what happens to her? Well, I haven't gotten that far, but
11 suffice it to say, she's damn funny. She's also endearing,
12 clever, charming, and resourceful. OK, go with me, the
13 play's finished. It's brilliant, of course. It gets published in
14 a snap, of course, and they're holding auditions, so of
15 course I show up — I mean, could there be a better part
16 for me? I wrote it for myself! Alright, mister or madame
17 director, here I come! "Next!" Uh, excuse me? I must have
18 misheard. This is the play about the thirty-five year-old,
19 tall, curly brown-haired, sarcastic Jewish girl, right?
20 "Thank, you. Next!"
21   So, back to the drawing board — I'd make the
22 character even more specific — for particular plot points,
23 she must be five-foot-ten. Chubby, hazel eyes, and right-
24 handed. I'd show up at auditions, all confident, and
25 "Next!" *More* specific, you say. Alright, my next Tony-
26 award-winning play stars a thirty-five year old, five-foot-
27 ten, chubby, brown-haired, sarcastic, hazel-eyed, size ten-
28 footed, Jewish girl with a birthmark on her right bicep, a
29 scar on her chin, two piercings in her left ear, and a
30 Siberian husky who answers to Sydney. "Next!" The dog
31 or just me? "Next!" I swear to you, I'm not kidding. I can
32 see it now.
33   I'm really tempted to just write it and see what
34 happens. I never really wanted to be a playwright, but
35 necessity is the mother of invention, they say. So I guess

1   it's true, talent and art don't mean squat next to looks. In
2   fact, as I talk to you, a nice, receptive, good-looking
3   audience in *(Insert name of city where monologue is being*
4   *performed)*, you might be thinking to yourself, "Hey, she
5   doesn't look at all like she says she looks. She's too hard
6   on herself. She's not chubby. She doesn't have a scar!
7   And that's a golden retriever, not a husky." Well, thank
8   you very much. I appreciate it, and so does Daisy, here.
9   But, just know, I didn't write this monologue. And the girl,
10   that is, the exceptional woman, who did is not here
11   tonight. Not that she didn't want to be. She just wasn't
12   cast. Her loss, I guess.

Leaving Ernesto
by SuzAnne C. Cole

1 *Casey, all makeup, hairspray, and spike heels, sits*
2 *uncomfortably in a standard wooden chair facing the audience.*
3 *Staring blankly into an imaginary mirror, she fusses with her*
4 *hair, checks her lipstick, and pictures herself as a*
5 Cosmopolitan *cover girl. Casey speaks candidly — and with*
6 *delicious double-meaning — about leaving Ernesto. It is not until*
7 *the final surprising line, however, that we learn what leaving*
8 *Ernesto really means!*
9

10 **CASEY:** I can't decide whether to stay with Ernesto or
11 not. We've been together so long, it's gonna be hard to
12 leave. But lately ... I find myself craving something
13 different. You know what I mean? Months go by, you're
14 mostly happy, then one day, bam, you wake up and think,
15 "This just isn't working anymore." Well, that's me.
16   Life with Ernesto has never been easy. He's expensive,
17 for one thing. Real expensive. Christmas, birthday, and
18 little "happy" presents had better be top drawer, or I
19 might as well not bother. Ernesto is my indulgence. And
20 ... mostly, he's been worth it. He's proud, did I say that?
21 And very prickly. Can't abide criticism. I can't tell you how
22 often I've gone home from one of our rendezvous with my
23 tongue practically bleeding 'cause I've bitten back so
24 many comments. Things I could get away with saying to a
25 girlfriend ... or even my husband. But I don't try them with
26 Ernesto. No, ma'am, I've learned better.
27   But, nobody else has ever known exactly what's right
28 for me except him. My fate's in his hands every time we
29 meet. And almost always, I'm really happy ... afterwards.

1 So, why am I thinking about leaving? For the last few
2 months, he's been showing up late for our dates. Not
3 terribly late, just ten minutes here, twenty minutes there.
4 Probably exercising his power. But last week, he flat stood
5 me up. I went to his place at our prearranged time and he
6 wasn't there. I hung around for an hour before I accepted
7 he wasn't coming. Oh, he claimed he totally forgot. But I
8 can't believe that. Not after all our times together.
9   If I were smart, I wouldn't leave him until I had his
10 replacement lined up ... But that's risky. He'd know
11 somehow — the look in my eyes, the sheen of my hair, the
12 smile on my lips. It's always been easier to fool everybody
13 else than it is to fool him. And when he guesses, then
14 what? I don't think he'd be violent ... but he always has
15 those sharp German scissors in his hand. I think I'll just
16 call and leave a message canceling our next tryst. Say my
17 husband's been transferred to a foreign country. We're
18 moving so soon, I don't even have time to say good-bye.
19 'Course, then I'll have to stay out of that part of town
20 forever.
21   Damn! Where am I going to find another hairdresser as
22 good as Ernesto?

Femonologues
by Jill Morley

1 *Missy, a breezy but vulnerable young woman, is a hopeless*
2 *dreamer who finds herself in a downward spiral filled with*
3 *disturbing undertones of self-worth. She is trapped in the drab*
4 *reality of poverty, the hardship of trailer park life, and an*
5 *abusive relationship with a dim-witted boyfriend, Earl. Here,*
6 *Missy is "hungry" to conjure up a magical world of beauty and*
7 *excitement thinking about a trip to Las Vegas, and imagines*
8 *that all that glitters really is gold.*
9
10 MISSY: Earl? Earl?? Did ya fix the carburetor yet? I'm
11 hungry. Well, why not? OK, OK. Smoke yer cigarette.
12 Figure it out. I can't wait till we get to Vegas, Earl! I heard
13 the restaurants are open twenty-four hours and every
14 meal is two ninety-nine! Sometimes one ninety-nine! And
15 that includes drinks. Alcoholic beverages! Yeah, beers.
16 Beers too! You'll get your beers, Earl. But, I'm gonna drink
17 them Pink Lady's with them pretty umbrellas stickin' out,
18 like the celebrities. I can too! Sebastion Shoemaker says
19 I look like Rita Hayworth. So what! He can see real good
20 with his other one. Would ya look at that cloud. It looks
21 like a giant slot machine. I'll bet it's a sign. Oh, my god,
22 Earl, we're gonna be rich! Oh, I can't wait! Know what I'm
23 gonna do? I'm gonna buy buckets of marigolds and
24 plant'em all around our trailer. Won't it look nice? What do
25 you mean, "Better'n that"? What's better'n livin' on a bed
26 of gold? Somethin' nobody can take from ya. I could look
27 at 'em every day to remind me how rich I am. Water 'em,
28 smell 'em, feel their soft petals — watch 'em grow ... A
29 Jaguar? Yeah, that would be good, too. But how can ya

1   think about Jaguars when ya can't even fix the carburetor
2   on a Maverick? Are ya done with yer cigarette, Earl? Earl??
3   I'm hungry.

Ten Pounds
by Kerri Kochanski

1 *Renee, an attractive, self-confident young woman with a fervent*
2 *sense of purpose, is a workout addict! Although she is perfectly*
3 *proportioned and well-toned, Renee is constantly in motion as*
4 *she struggles to keep herself fit and trim. Here she faces an*
5 *imaginary full-length mirror and jogs furiously in place with*
6 *exercise weights, looking for the self-perfection that she so*
7 *desperately seeks.*
8

9 RENEE: *Ten* pounds. I need to lose *ten* pounds ...Well I
10 don't need to really ... But I would like to ... I would *like*
11 to lose ten pounds ... Liking to and *needing* to are different
12 things ... If you would like to, then it is something you
13 would like to do ... Things like fishing or ice skating —
14 things that you always seem to think about. Year after
15 year. But never get around to ...
16 *(She continues to jog.)* **Needing**, though ... Some people
17 need to do things ... *(Thinks.)*
18 Like filling out taxes ... Tax *forms*, I mean ...
19 I don't *need* to do it ... so I don't know ...
20 *(Clarifies.)* I mean I *need* to do it ... But my boyfriend
21 does it for me ... Some things you need to do, but you can
22 get other people — *(Grows dissatisfied.)*
23 Not *weight loss*, though ...
24 *(Quoting)* "You need to lose weight yourself ..." *For*
25 yourself ... Not for anybody else ... *(Thinks.)*
26 Well, maybe your doctor ... If you *needed* to ... But
27 then you would have a purpose you see ... ?
28 *(Weighs the options.)* "Heart attack" or "diet."
29 "Diabetes" or "diet."

1   People that don't *need* ... Have less motivation ...
2   *(She stops. Grabs exercise weight from floor.)* **This**
3   **weight ... This weight weighs ten pounds ... Ten pounds of**
4   **fat ... That is on my body — and doesn't** *have* **to be ...**
5   **If I could just get rid of it ...**
6   *(She considers. Throws weight to the side. Resumes*
7   *jogging.)* **But I don't** *need* **to ...**
8   *(Thinks about it.)* **I** *want* **to ... I really want to ...**
9   *(She suddenly stops, realizing.)* **But I don't** *need* **to ...**
10   *(She looks down at body, then back up at audience.*
11   *Wonders.)* **Do I?**

Acceptance Speech
by Deanna Riley

1 *Brooke, a perky, take-charge mother, wife, daughter-in-law, and*
2 *professional colleague, is being honored at an awards banquet.*
3 *Standing poised in front of a podium and clutching her small*
4 *plaque, Brooke's spirits soar as her acceptance speech builds to*
5 *a wickedly funny climax that leaves a stunned audience*
6 *squirming nervously on the edges of their seats.*

7

8 BROOKE: I want to thank the Academy of Women in the
9 Middle for this honor. Although I know I have earned every
10 bit of this prestigious award, I do want to thank the people
11 who helped make this possible.
12 *(To the heavens)* Mom, I wish you were here to see this.
13 You wouldn't believe it. Not about the award, but that I
14 actually ironed this outfit. See, I remembered something.
15 *(To her daughter in audience)* First, I could not have won
16 this honor without my teenage daughter, Courtney, who
17 ignored her curfew and turned off her cell phone when
18 convenient and made my hair go gray in a single evening
19 when she went on a date with a college senior to a frat
20 party. Thank you Courtney, and you're still grounded.
21 *(To her father-in-law in audience)* I want to thank my
22 father-in-law, Frank, who insisted he could recover
23 completely from shoulder replacement surgery in only four
24 days. All seventy-two year-olds recover faster than twenty-
25 something professional athletes.
26 *(As the father-in-law)* "It's a medical known fact.
27 Experience beats youth every time."
28 *(To her father-in-law in audience)* In your imagination.
29 Please don't think I believe you're senile. You're not.

1   You're stubborn. I'm really not mad about sleeping on the
2   couch at your house for two weeks to take care of you
3   because you refused the nursing help the doctor
4   recommended. Not even annoyed.
5   *(To her husband in audience)* I am a little ticked at my
6   husband, Stan, who took that opportunity to go on three
7   business trips. Guess who is sleeping on the couch now,
8   dear?
9   *(To committee members in audience)* I want to thank the
10   high school prom committee who insisted that building an
11   entrance that replicated the parting of the Red Sea would
12   be fun and easy. Thank you for twenty-one weekends of
13   "fun" and "easy" that computed to forty-five seconds in
14   my daughter's life. It was impressive. Overkill, but
15   impressive.
16   *(To fellow workers in audience)* I want to acknowledge
17   those guys at work who think women are getting all the
18   breaks. Would any of you want to trade places with me?
19   Really?
20   *(To female colleagues in audience)* And let's not forget
21   those female colleagues — ah, that would be you,
22   Rebecca — who think there's only room for one woman on
23   the promotion track. Thanks so much for not sharing.
24   *(She regroups.)* I'm sorry. Let me refocus here and talk
25   about the folks who really matter, who truly helped me get
26   this award. The people who make being a
27   mom/wife/employee/daughter-in-law/baker/candlestick
28   maker/Indian chief all worthwhile.
29   *(To female colleagues in audience)* Thanks to Diane who
30   jumped over secretary to executive and still held the door
31   open for other women. But shut the door and let me cry in
32   her office so no one could see.
33   *(To fellow workers in audience)* Thanks to my colleagues
34   at work — male and female — who covered for me during
35   an important presentation when I had to pick up my sick

1   kid with a stomach virus from school. And then forgave
2   me when I spread that flu to everyone in our department.
3   *(To a friend in audience)* I want to thank friends like
4   Jackie for allowing me to vent and move on instead of
5   exploding like a shaken soda or stagnating like those
6   breakfast dishes in the sink — which I will get to.
7   *(To her father-in-law in audience)* I thank my father-in-law
8   for loving me just because I love his son.
9   *(To committee members in audience)* I want to thank that
10   crazy-ambitious prom committee for caring enough about
11   my kid and all the other teenagers to make a special night.
12   *(To her daughter in audience)* I thank my daughter who
13   will still give me a hug and kiss in front of her friends.
14   *(To her husband in audience)* I want to thank my
15   husband for bringing me a glass of wine or a bowl of ice
16   cream without asking, and knowing which one I needed.
17   *(To the heavens)* And I want to thank you, Mom, for
18   giving me the tools to handle this. I didn't choose all this,
19   but I have it. Wish you were here to see this. This award
20   is for you.
21   *(To the audience at large)* And for me. I deserve it. Thank
22   you.

Skylar
by Samara Siskind

1 *Gloria, a sensitive and introspective young woman dealing with*
2 *loss, has just come from visiting her mother's gravesite.*
3 *Struggling with the loss of her mother, she is also still haunted*
4 *by the sudden death of Skylar, her infant daughter, several*
5 *years earlier. Gloria's poignant memories awaken her once*
6 *again to the harsh reality of life's happy entrances and sad exits*
7 *that have become ... just another routine visit.*
8

9 GLORIA: I went to the cemetery today.
10   It was a routine visit. I cleaned the headstone.
11 Arranged my flowers. Arranged them again. I sat. I cried.
12 Told a few mundane stories spanning time since my last
13 visit. Kept a steady eye out for raccoons. One time a
14 raccoon was prancing around like he owned the place.
15 Perhaps he was visiting a loved one. An elderly gentleman
16 named Fred who would leave apple cores for him in the
17 backyard.
18   I hate that it's become routine ... relieved the pain is
19 only a fraction of what it used to be. I miss her. My eyes
20 scan all the other headstones in view. I calculate how old
21 everyone was when they passed. I don't know why I do
22 this. A husband and wife are side by side ... one year
23 apart. That year was probably an eternity to her. Maybe
24 not. Maybe they made a pact ... after one of them passed
25 the other had to go to Tahiti. This is what goes through my
26 head.
27   I stand. Say goodbye. Cry again. Arrange the flowers.
28 I leave.
29   On the way out I see it. I stop. I always do. Just

1   reading it makes my heart break over and over. Skylar
2   Brooke. Lived eighty-six days. 1999-2000. There is a little
3   butterfly engraved. And the quote. The quote gets me
4   every time. "You with the stars in your eyes." I sit. I visit
5   Skylar.
6   I've been coming here for the past four years. Since
7   she was supposed to be three. Every year I imagine her
8   growing older. Her with the stars in her eyes. Today she
9   would be seven. I imagine she must be lonely here,
10   surrounded by all of these older people. People who had
11   the chance to live what most would consider full lives. I
12   think about where she is, in what form. Is she still a baby?
13   An adorable second grader? I try to picture her. I see
14   ponytails and barrettes. Freckles. One missing front
15   tooth.
16   I think about my mom and wonder if she's met Skylar.
17   Is she holding her in her arms, comforting her cries ... or
18   sipping tea at her make-believe tea party. My mom always
19   was the best babysitter.
20   I leave one small bud for her. For Skylar.
21   I arrange it again so it's near the butterfly.
22   Just another routine visit.

Raccoon Ball
by Jeff Goode

1 *A frustrated young girl stands with a baseball bat in her hand*
2 *and struggles to reconcile her love of baseball and the disgust*
3 *she feels for Jason, her cruel and disturbed brother who has*
4 *been playing "Raccoon Ball" in the backyard. She wavers*
5 *between anguish and hope before deciding to take matters into*
6 *her own hands before her brother becomes even more sadistic.*
7 *Her cunning plan of action involves an enticing offer she hopes*
8 *Jason will not refuse.*
9
10 **YOUNG GIRL:** I love raccoons. They are so cute. I used to
11 love baseball. *(Sadly)* But that was before the raccoons. My
12 dad always used to play catch with me and my brother
13 Jason in the backyard every day after work. Even if he got
14 home late, he always had time to let us practice batting
15 balls around.
16   I was always way better at it than my brother. He's
17 horrible. My dad says it's because I have the love of the
18 game. And Jason just loves pounding things he finds in
19 the yard.
20   So his bat is always chipped up. Or covered in bugs.
21 And he never practices hard like I do. *(She takes a practice*
22 *swing.)* But we don't get to play as much since my mom
23 died. And my dad had his thing. *(She makes "Dad is crazy"*
24 *gesture.)*
25   They sent me and Jason to live with our grandparents.
26 And they live in the country, so now our backyard has
27 raccoons. Which are the most completely adorable animals
28 I have ever seen in person.
29   They have built-in masks, like little bandits. But they

1   don't steal things, except what you already threw away.
2   Which drives Grandpa crazy, because some nights they
3   come up on the back porch and knock over the garbage.
4   Well, every night. He gets pretty upset about that.
5   Grandma doesn't mind so much, though, because she
6   says they're clean animals, because raccoons always wash
7   their food before they eat it. Which is more than Jason.
8   But actually — did you know? — the reason they do it
9   is because raccoons don't have any saliva of their own. So
10   they have to rinse off their food before they eat it, so it's
11   moist and soft in their mouth.
12   But now that Grandpa got those special locks to put
13   on the garbage cans, they can't get into them any more.
14   So I started feeding them with whatever I didn't eat from
15   dinner, so they don't go hungry. I don't need as much as
16   Grandma tries to feed me anyway.
17   Every night, I put out a plate of leftovers on the back
18   porch. And a little glass of water, in case they want to eat
19   it there. Then when the raccoons come up on the porch —
20   my brother jumps out with his baseball bat and pounds
21   them on the head. Then he pours lighter fluid on them and
22   sets them on fire. He's horrible.
23   I told him the president says it's wrong to kill raccoons
24   because we're in a culture of life. But he just says, "Some
25   things need killing," and does it anyway. So now when I
26   think about baseball it kinda makes me sick to my
27   stomach.
28   But I saved up my allowance and got this new game-
29   station cartridge for my brother. *(She takes out a video game
30   cartridge.)* And tonight I'm gonna leave it out on the back
31   porch for him. With a glass of soda in case he wants to
32   play it right there.
33   And I'm gonna see if I can restore my love of the game.
34   *(She takes a slow, careful practice swing.)*

Running Giraffe
by Laura E. Cotton

1 *Alyssa, an attractive young woman with a bubbly, sweet, and*
2 *sensitive nature, takes her nieces to a birthday party. While*
3 *sipping some punch, she sees a familiar figure lurking in the*
4 *background. A clown approaches her and sets off a tense,*
5 *disturbing, and frightening flashback as Alyssa is forced to*
6 *relive a past nightmare with another clown when she was in*
7 *the sixth grade.*
8
9 **ALYSSA: Stop! Stop right there! Get away from me! You**
10 **... you ... clown!**
11 *(Brief pause, she looks at the Clown.)* **I'm sorry. I don't**
12 **mean to be rude, it's just ... it's just ... I hate clowns.**
13 **They scare the beejeezees outta me. I mean, it's nothing**
14 **against you or your profession or anything. I just don't like**
15 **them. I wouldn't have come if I'd known this was a ... a ...**
16 ***clown* party. I mean, I thought kids didn't have those**
17 **anymore. I thought little kids today liked Barney and ... I**
18 **don't know ... Elmo. Isn't Elmo big now? And I was just**
19 **trying to be nice, taking my sister's kids to this. I wasn't**
20 **trying to overcome, you know, a lifelong fear.**
21 *(Looks up, sees the Clown's face.)* **Oh. You look sad now.**
22 **Or is that just your face?**
23 *(Waits a moment, no answer.)* **Not real talkative, are you?**
24 **Or are you a mime too?**
25 *(Brief pause)* **I really ... I really don't mean to offend you.**
26 **It's just ... Well ...**
27 *(Takes a deep breath, then stands up.)* **When I was little,**
28 **every year my school had this Halloween parade. Everyone**
29 **would dress up, you know, in costumes, and the different**

1   grades would walk through the school, showing off
2   throughout the day. It was my favorite day of the year. My
3   mom always made me the best costumes. I was kinda tall
4   so she managed to come up with some pretty creative
5   ideas. One year I was the Leaning Tower of Pisa. Another
6   year a string bean. It was always so exciting ...
7   *(Beat.)* Until ... Until ... sixth grade. I was a giraffe that
8   year. School had just let out. I was walking home, still in
9   my costume. It was October, but it was still kinda hot in
10   there. I was just walking along when ... When I heard this
11   whistling behind me. You know, the way men whistle at
12   girls they kinda like? That way. I turned around and there
13   was this clown behind me. Following me. With this huge,
14   phony, red grin on his face. Like the devil or ... the joker.
15   You know, from those Batman movies?
16   *(Beat.)* I didn't know what to do. So I just started
17   running. As fast as I could. Running through the woods in
18   my giraffe costume. I felt like a real giraffe. A giraffe who
19   was being hunted. I looked behind me once and I didn't
20   see him. But I just kept running.
21   *(Beat.)* When I got home, I sat down on my bed and
22   cried. A few hours later, I turn on the T.V. I'm watching
23   some cartoons or something, when this news reporter
24   interrupts the program with a special report. A picture
25   comes on the screen. A picture of ...
26   *(Hesitant)* The clown. The one who was following me.
27   The reporter says he attacked a little girl. A little girl at
28   my school. And he almost killed her.
29   *(Beat.)* So that's why. Why I don't like clowns, I mean.
30   It's nothing personal. It's just ... well ...
31   *(Shoos him to go away.)* **Go away!**

Nuts
by Kerri Kochanski

1   *Chloe, a spirited young woman struggling to control her weight,*
2   *is clearly at the end of her rope when she discovers that her*
3   *boyfriend has brought a bag of nuts into the house. She*
4   *suspects that he is trying to sabotage her diet routine by*
5   *tempting her with fattening foods, and makes no secret of her*
6   *sense of outrage and betrayal.*
7
8   **CHLOE:** *Nuts?!* **You're bringing nuts into this house ... !**
9   **What** *are* **you ... if not stupid ... If not — totally**
10 *insane* **...**
11   *(She holds up bag of nuts.)* **These have calories! And I**
12 **can't have these calories — Clogging up my cabinets!** *(She*
13 *seethes.)* **Get them out of here then ... Get — it**
14 *out* **...**
15   **And while you're at it —** *You* **get out of here, too ...**
16 *(She can't believe him.)* **You** *know* **I am on a diet ... Didn't I**
17 **tell you I am "on a diet"?**
18   **So I don't want things like** *nuts* **... I don't** *need* **things**
19 **like** *nuts* **... Sitting here ...** *Tempting* **me in this house ... !**
20   *(Stopping)* **Maybe you can control yourself — but**
21 **I ... ? I** *can't* **control myself ... I see these nuts —** *(She looks*
22 *at bag. Begins stuffing her mouth crazily with nuts.)* **And I feel**
23 **like a** *squirrel* **... Like a squirrel — Foraging for the winter**
24 **... A squirrel stuffing her cheeks — Until she cannot stuff**
25 **them anymore —.**
26   *(Stopping, controlling herself)* *That* **is how I feel —** *that* **is**
27 **what I'll do — so when you tempt me ... You are just**
28 **making it worse. You are just making — An already** *bad*
29 **situation** *worse.*

1   So I can't have you around me. If you are not willing to
2   respect my boundaries —
3   *(Listens for a moment, then)* I don't *care* whose house it
4   is. *You* pay the food bill ...
5   *(She thinks about it.)* You should be *glad* ... ! Glad that
6   I am saving you so much *money* ... Because you don't
7   have to buy things ... Things like *nuts* ... Which can get
8   *expensive* ...
9   So it all works out in the end. I save you money on
10   *food*, thus saving money for the *house*, you put this money
11   toward the *house*, in the form of a *mortgage* bill ... So
12   really *I* am paying for the mortgage ... *That's* the way it
13   is ...
14   *(She is done with him.)* Go, you and your nuts — Get
15   out of here!
16   *(She throws the bag.)* The door is closing. It's closed.
17   And I'm locking the cabinets!

Murder to What Degree?
by Deborah Maddox

1   *In this disturbing account of "Murder to What Degree?" a troubled*
2   *teenage girl has endured an unbearable life of constant abuse and*
3   *brutality from her insensitive and drunken father. Eventually, this*
4   *intolerable condition leads to an irreversible descent into the pit of*
5   *numbing fear ... and in an act of hopeless desperation the*
6   *teenager shoots and kills her father. Here, she justifies her actions*
7   *to a police psychologist who is interviewing her.*
8
9   TEENAGER: Angry? Anger was just part of it. I grew up
10   with the nice house and the nice cars. I even had my own
11   credit cards. I guess you could say I had everything. That's
12   what my friends thought anyway. But ... I also had my dad.
13   Every day. Maybe it was his work that got to him. I don't
14   know. What I do know is that the only time my dad showed
15   me love ... was after he beat me. Oh yeah. He would come
16   home drunk, bouncing off the walls. He had this rage
17   inside of him. He always had a crazy look in his eyes when
18   he was drunk. He would shove me around, yelling at me ...
19   telling me that everything was always my fault. And he'd
20   get this close to my face. He loved that, because when he
21   was close, he could see my fear. My whole body would
22   shake. Yeah, he loved that. I can still smell him. I'm lucky
23   that hair grows back. Do you know how much it hurts to
24   have your hair pulled out of your head by the handful?
25   Yeah, I hated him, every single day. Put yourself in my
26   shoes. Wouldn't you have shot him too?

Chapter 3
Comic Mirrors:
Funhouse and Fantasy

"There is delight in singing, though
none hear ... except the singer."
— Elizabeth Barrett Browning,
The Cry of the Human

These delightful characters from full-length playscripts are by turns filled with fun or fantasy, mirroring the patchwork patterns of ordinary women who sing their songs to the tune of choices made long ago. The songs are lyrical when they soar skyward and are filled with a spirit of compassion and humanity. The songs fall back to earth just as quickly in the helpless laughter of comic misadventures or tragic missteps that mirror painful regret and dashed hopes. The playwrights here make no attempt to disguise their pointed thrusts, but the funhouse mirror often conceals or distorts what is comic and what is semi-tragic in the day-to-day struggles reflected in these irrepressible character portraits.

The solo singers are, for the most part, simple women engaged in non-heroic actions who speak in frank and honest voices. They share a number of basic impulses — fear, loneliness, and self-delusion — that are treated alternately with comic glee or brittle satire. There is also a certain beauty and grace in these characters when they raise their voice in songs of defiance or rebellion to punctuate inner truths, using unvarnished language that is both arresting and alarming.

As you voice these songs, it is important to keep in mind that the texts have a dual impulse. Although some are decidedly comic, they may also have a dramatic undercurrent of grief, frustration, or sorrow. The focus here should be on the bubbling forces that surface in each character's lyrics so that you can isolate the basic elements that incite the comic or tragic impulse — whether it is the character's action, language, or situation.

Don't forget to look for the clues that identify the world in which these characters are living at this precise point in time as well.

In playing the character roles of fun and fantasy, you will need to be natural and spontaneous in both voice and body. There should be no exaggeration of the comic or tragic dimensions of the character portraits. In spite of the surface humor these characters exhibit, there is a submerged measure of personal dignity in each portrait that should be visible in performance. The brief introduction to each monologue suggests the raw slice-of-life circumstances that agitate or provoke the characters, and your audition blueprint should add a flavor and texture of simplicity and directness to reflect these ingredients in performance.

Special emphasis should also be paid to indicate how these characters are familiar to us. Bodily actions, gestures, and movement should reflect appropriate mannerisms or traits discovered in an analysis of the text. Don't forget to chart vocal and physical changes that appear to take place in each character as well. If you are sensitive to what you have discovered, your stage portrait will bear a remarkable resemblance to the monologue character, and your performance will be as believable as if what is happening in the text were an everyday event.

The Pyre
by Terri Campion

1   *Vicki Kearney is in her first hectic year of teaching third-grade*
2   *students. She is a young, passionate, and idealistic teacher*
3   *actively engaged in providing guidance and a sense of*
4   *direction to impressionable young students. Here, Vicki*
5   *strives to remain focused and positive as she prepares her*
6   *class for an unexpected school fire drill which has disrupted*
7   *her daily lesson plans.*
8
9   VICKI: OK, boys and girls. *Class?!* All eyes up front! As
10 you know, like our special guest of the week — Fire
11 Person Ms. Crawford — told you yesterday, it's Fire
12 Prevention Week. And I was just told, at the last
13 possible minute, that in ... *(She looks at the clock)* three
14 minutes we are going to have a fire drill. So, I need
15 everyone to close your notebooks for now. We'll come
16 back to our journal writing after lunch. But right now,
17 we need to *quietly* clear our desks. That means all
18 erasers, pencils, tissues, cell phones — everything must
19 disappear. Now, I'm going to close my eyes and count
20 to five, and when I open them I want to see clear desks
21 and thirty-three little angels sitting with their hands
22 folded. *(She covers her eyes.)* One. Two. Three. No
23 talking! Four. Five. Boys and girls are your desks clear?
24 *(She uncovers her eyes.)* Very nice. Now — calmly — we
25 will stand. *(She gestures with her hands for the students to*
26 *rise out of their desks.)* And starting with the first row —
27 Jason put your Palm Pilot inside your desk! This is a
28 drill. There is no actual fire, but if there were, we might
29 have all been burned to a crisp by now because some of

1   you refuse to let go of material possessions! Now! Single
2   file! First row, march! *Quiet* ... ly! Please. Thank you.
3   Follow behind Ms. Rippo's class, I'll be right there, and I
4   want to hear nothing but excellent reports on your
5   behavior. *(Beat.)* Aren't they cute?

Women Alone
by Christopher Woods

1   *Francine, a sleek-looking and wildly successful food critic,*
2   *enters wearing an evening gown and a glimmering tiara.*
3   *Known as the "First Lady of Taste," she takes a few graceful*
4   *bows to the audience and kisses an American flag that hangs*
5   *on a stand downstage. What follows is a sparkling portrait of*
6   *a woman who bristles with dark humor, but who also knows*
7   *a number of uncomfortable truths that she serves from her*
8   *"Freedom Buffet" tray.*
9
10   **FRANCINE: Good evening! Thank you so very much!**
11   **Good evening to you all. And you know, it goes without**
12   **saying, Francine considers each and every one of you**
13   **her best friend. But you already know that, don't you?**
14   **Yes, I thought so.** *(Slight pause.)* **Oh yes, I can feel your**
15   **love. I am standing in the shower of your love.** *(She takes*
16   *another bow, then blows several kisses to the audience. She*
17   *then blows a kiss to the flag.)*
18   **It's always such a joy to meet with my many readers**
19   **in person. I want to reach out and touch every one of**
20   **you.** *(Sighs.)* **But there's no time for that. No, tonight I**
21   **have something very special to share with you. If you**
22   **read my columns, you know that there is nothing else in**
23   **my life as important as food.** *Nothing!* **Food is my life.**
24   **Take it away, and there would be no Francine.**
25   *(She goes to the flag and stands at attention.)* **As an**
26   **American, I feel that it is the sign of a mature society to**
27   **place such importance on food. Isn't it true, friends? We**
28   ***love* food. And we *need* food. But tell me something.**
29   **Don't we also like to decorate it? Yes! And aren't we**

1   fascinated by the visual appearance of food? Of course we
2   are!
3   But listen to Francine when she says there is an even
4   larger picture to consider. Tonight, I would like to discuss
5   my philosophy about dining out. Specifically, I want to talk
6   to you about cafeterias. *(Slight pause, then brightly)* And
7   *freedom!* In my mind, dining out and freedom of choice go
8   hand in hand. As Americans — proud ones, I hope — it is
9   our basic right to dine in a place of our choosing. The
10   Founding Fathers told us this.
11   *(She walks into the audience, shaking and kissing hands.)*
12   Oh, it's so good to be out among the people. My readers.
13   Sitting at my desk, way up in the editorial tower, it would
14   be easy to forget about all of you. The *little* people. So
15   many critics do. But I am here to tell you that Francine
16   Stott del Ray will never forget the little people. You can
17   depend on me. Now, let's join hands, shall we? That's
18   right. Just take the hand of the person sitting next to you.
19   *(Appears to be listening to someone in the audience.)* What is
20   that, dear? You don't know the man sitting next to you?
21   Well, that is exactly why I am asking you to hold hands.
22   *Feel good* about the person sitting next to you. Smile at
23   them. Keep holding hands. Are we ready now? I hope so.
24   Let's concentrate for a moment. Can you feel it? The
25   power? *(Louder) The power?* Yes, I thought you would.
26   Now, let's try a little experiment. Would you like that?
27   Good. Close your eyes. That's right, close your eyes.
28   *Everyone!* No cheating back there! No, no, no! Now, is
29   everyone ready? Think of a word with me. Concentrate.
30   The word is *cafeteria.* Yes! *Cafeteria!* *(Enraptured)* Yes!
31   Please, say it along with me. Everyone, now. *Cafeteria.*
32   Now, louder. *Cafeteria!* Wonderful, wonderful! Do you feel
33   the power? Of course you do! The power is in the word
34   itself, *cafeteria.*
35   *(Slight pause. She frees her hands and motions for others to*

1   *do the same. She returns to the stage, adopts a lecture pose.)* I
2   learned this power early on. As a child, I was already
3   thinking about freedom. And freedom of choice. I
4   remember Sunday afternoons, going to the cafeteria with
5   my parents after church services. Our cafeteria was a
6   warm place, filled with goodwill. *(She can wrap herself in the*
7   *flag if desired.)* It was also a democratic place. Why, you
8   could see Catholics, Protestants, and Jews all in a line.
9   Oh, we hadn't brought home half of Asia at that point. Nor
10 do I remember Moslems. But if they had come, we would
11 have made room!
12   *(Suddenly, she begins walking on tiptoe, pretending to*
13 *push a cafeteria tray.)* I stood on my toes to view the feast
14 that awaited us. God bless the preview line! Even then I
15 was a culinary explorer. I would try a different salad every
16 Sunday. I must confess, I was always on the lookout for a
17 new salad friend. Oh, Papa would be a bear if he didn't get
18 his Waldorf salad. Mama loved her Jell-O molds. When
19 Grandma was still alive, she would make a beeline for the
20 stewed prunes.
21   *(Sighs heavily.)* I'm sure it was my mother's fondness
22 for Jell-O that influenced me most. That is how I acquired
23 my reverence for Jell-O. *(Shudders with delight.)* Which is
24 why, when I was asked to speak here tonight, I considered
25 talking to you about Jell-O. But I realized the possibilities
26 were endless, without even broaching the molds
27 themselves.
28   *(She pushes the imaginary tray toward the flag.)* So I
29 decided to talk about food and freedom. *(Slight pause.)* I
30 never passed through the cafeteria line without saying a
31 prayer of thanks. *(She kisses the flag.)* Didn't I live in a
32 country where cafeterias began? Where freedom of choice
33 was guaranteed? And, by God, still is?
34   *(She puts down the imaginary tray.)* Please, join me.
35 *(She bows her head in prayer, then beats her heart religiously.)*

1   What can I tell you of the desserts of my childhood? Each
2   was a sugary friend, and I have remained faithful to them
3   all. As my readers, it will interest you to know that my very
4   first writing was done in my private, white leatherette
5   dessert diary. I filled each page with secret wishes. An
6   extra helping of strawberry shortcake! A house made of
7   pineapple pie!
8   *(From this point on, she becomes more manic.)* **And**
9   always, Jell-O. Because you see, Jell-O can be a salad or
10   a dessert. In the best meals, Jell-O is like bookends.
11   *(She produces a cake pan. Inside it, an American flag made*
12   *of blue and red Jell-O, with whipped cream for stripes and small*
13   *marshmallows for stars. She shows it to the audience, shaking*
14   *it to make the flag jiggle a bit.)* **See what I brought to share**
15   with you? It is my very own recipe, "Flag in the Wind."
16   Watch it! See for yourself! Isn't it marvelous? I go through
17   at least three of these a week. I can't be away from my
18   Jell-O flag friends for very long.
19   *(She approaches the audience. She scoops out a star and*
20   *eats it.)* **Sometimes, as I eat the stars, I count them.** *(She*
21   *eats another star.)* **And I name them.** *(Eats another.)* **Ah,**
22   **Nebraska! Mmmmm, so good!** *(She offers a star to an*
23   *audience member.)* **Please, won't you eat New Jersey?** *(She*
24   *pulls out plastic spoons from her dress.)* **Oh, there's enough**
25   for everyone. Ours is a big country.
26   *(Ad libbing is allowed at this point. Then, she returns to the*
27   *flag area.)* **Please, allow me to conclude my remarks. It is**
28   so good to be an American. Freedom of choice is what
29   made this country what it is. It was in cafeterias that I
30   learned about democracy. Isn't it freedom of choice that
31   allows a person to eat a vegetable plate? Or two kinds of
32   meat on the same plate? Of course it is!
33   Just last week, I saw a woman in line ahead of me at
34   the cafeteria. For her patriotic meal, she had chosen five
35   salads. I pushed my tray closer and I said to that woman,

1   *"This* is what America is all about! This is why our young
2   men must go to war, to make the world safe for
3   cafeterias!" *(Triumphantly)* Cafeterias, friends, are constant
4   reminders of freedom. We can choose. Therefore, we are!
5   Happy dining! Happy freedom! I love you all! God bless!

Don't Call Me Loretta
by Nancy Gall-Clayton

1   *It is just a few minutes before quitting time for gritty Loretta,*
2   *a gutsy waitress with a sour disposition tonight, when an*
3   *unwelcome trucker stumbles into the small, aging diner.*
4   *Before he can place an order, Loretta quickly turns the table*
5   *on him and hands the trucker a full-menu of razor-sharp*
6   *barbs that makes this late-night order a fun serving chock-full*
7   *of humor.*
8
9   LORETTA: If I were you, I wouldn't get too comfortable,
10   and I wouldn't take too much time reading that menu
11   neither. We don't have half that stuff — ever — and we
12   sure don't have it now. We're closing in five, mister.
13   Five. I'm the last one here, and I don't linger for nobody.
14   If the president himself walked in here right now, I'd tell
15   him to leave. That's right. When it's five till nine, it's five
16   till nine. Get it? I'm focusing on the nine. The only thing
17   I will happily sell you right now is a cup of coffee. If
18   that's what you want, fine, just say so, and don't act
19   like this here's the Holiday Inn. The coffee's going on
20   two hours old, and it'll cost you one dollar plus whatever
21   you tip me for taking care of you when it's five minutes
22   till closing. Which should be at least fifty cents, if you
23   want my opinion. Anything less than fifty cents would be
24   an insult, and you wouldn't want to insult me, now,
25   would you? A dollar would be nice. There's no law
26   against the tip being the same as the bill, you know. You
27   could even tip bigger than the bill. I seen it happen once.
28   But not to me.
29   Now, if you're really starving and you can't get by on

1   just a cup of coffee, I guess I could give you a pickle. We
2   keep them in brine, and all I have to do is fish one out for
3   you. They cost a dollar, too. Other than that, everything's
4   put up. So, one black coffee and a dill pickle — that's what
5   I'm offering. That's all I'm offering. What'll it be, mister?

Nice Tie
by Rich Orloff

1   *An unidentified single and self-confident woman sits quietly*
2   *on a plush barstool late at night and gives serious thought to*
3   *the offer of a complimentary cocktail made by a man seated*
4   *next to her. This seemingly innocent invitation quickly takes*
5   *on mock-serious undertones when the woman unexpectedly*
6   *responds with a stream of incredible comic complications that*
7   *might result if she were to accept his flattering offer.*

8

9   WOMAN: Can you buy me a drink, you ask. Oh, I don't
10   know. First you buy me a drink, and then you ask for my
11   phone number, and I figure what the hell, so I give it to
12   you. If you don't call me, I'm disappointed. If you do call
13   me, we go out, and either I don't like you, or I like you
14   and you don't like me. And I'm disappointed. Or we do
15   like each other, and we go out some more, and things
16   become pretty wonderful — great passion, revealing
17   conversations, compatible neuroses — but I discover I
18   want more than you can give. And I'm disappointed.
19   Or we stay with it, and we get closer and closer and
20   more dependent on each other, which gives us the
21   strength to go through periods of mutual doubts, and
22   things said in anger that we'll pretend to forget but
23   which will come up again during the post-natal
24   depression I'll have after the birth of our first child. *If* we
25   get married, that is, and Lord knows how many friends
26   I'll lose because they like me but they're just not
27   comfortable around you.
28   After our second child, the unresolved conflicts we
29   buried for the sake of our marriage will propel you into

1   a torrid affair, either with someone you work with or, God
2   forbid, one of my few friends who is comfortable around
3   you. I'll try to forgive you, eventually, by which point both
4   our children will be in intensive therapy.
5   The divorce will be ugly, expensive, and I'll never be
6   able to trust men again, those who aren't frightened off by
7   my sagging features and two sadomasochistic children.
8   The kids'll blame me, of course, and I'll die alone ... I think
9   I'll pass on the drink.

Bad Dates
by Theresa Rebeck

1   *This intensely haunting one-woman script showcases a*
2   *bright, mature woman whose only good luck is attracting*
3   *bad dates. Connie has decided to re-enter the dating-go-round*
4   *circuit and paints a desolate self-portrait of romantic futility in*
5   *bold strokes of desperation, guilt, and comic lust that is clever*
6   *tongue-in-cheek humor.*
7

8   CONNIE: So, I'm like, OK, this is just a date that's not
9   going to work out. That's obvious, and it's not the end
10   of the world, and frankly, I didn't actually think the first
11   guy I went out with would be "the one for me" or
12   anything like that. I was just trying to go on a date. So
13   I'm OK with the fact that this is largely pretty stupid.
14   And then, there's actually a point in the evening where
15   having completely given up on this guy I sort of
16   perversely got interested in his story. He starts talking
17   about his ex-girlfriend. And the more he talks about her,
18   the clearer it becomes that he's still, really, kind of in
19   love with her. And the more I listen to him, the more I
20   realize that this is more or less a first date for him, too,
21   he's recently broken up with this woman he really loved,
22   and now he's trying to get back on the horse. And this
23   thought honestly makes me feel a little warmly toward
24   him, I sense that we are fellow-travelers. And so I say to
25   him, as a fellow-traveler, well, why did you break up?
26   And he tells me this story about how — that your
27   relationship with a person is like a movie. That when
28   you're in a relationship, you see the movie, in your head,
29   and that you need to see how the rest of the movie is

1 going to go. And he realized that he couldn't see where the
2 movie was going. He didn't know the end of the movie,
3 with this woman. So he had to break up with her. And he
4 looked so sad. Meanwhile, I'm listening to this, and trying
5 to understand, so I say, "What do you mean, a movie?"
6 And he goes through the whole thing again, about looking
7 for the end of the movie, and your life with someone, and
8 the relationship, and the end of the movie, so I say, you
9 mean like death? Looking for the end of the movie, you're
10 thinking about dying? And he says, "No no no, it's not
11 about death. It's about the End of the Movie." And we go
12 around in circles like that for a while, and finally I say to
13 him, I don't know, is it possible that you broke up with the
14 woman you loved because of some insane metaphor?

15 And then he got mad at me. I don't blame him. I
16 definitely was getting too personal. And I honestly had a
17 moment when I thought, if you're siding with the guy's ex-
18 girlfriend, it's not a good date. So then things were
19 uncomfortable, and they kind of went from bad to worse,
20 and by the end of the evening we were really annoyed with
21 each other, and I let him stick his tongue in my mouth,
22 anyway.

Service du Jour
by Gail Blanton

1   *Mandy, a seasoned "server" at church worship services,*
2   *enters briskly and mounts the raised platform that faces the*
3   *sanctuary. She directs her lines toward the back, as if a large,*
4   *standing-room-only crowd is anxiously waiting to be seated.*
5   *Mandy's* Service du Jour *menu of mayhem is an oddly*
6   *satiric torching of traditional worship services and lethally*
7   *funny liturgy.*
8

9   **MANDY: Excuse me, is everyone inside back there?**
10   **Everyone who was on the waiting list? Everyone whose**
11   **little palm-held reservation thingie lit up?**
12   **The little thing that flashed and** *(Pounces on the*
13   *pronunciation of "buzzed" as if it is an attack)* **buzzed and**
14   **scared the living daylights out of you? OK then. Julio,**
15   **tell the others outside that their wait will be one hour**
16   *(Insert the time your service is supposed to last).* *(Clears*
17   *throat.)* **More or less.**
18   **Good morning, ladies and gentlemen. My name is**
19   **Mandy, and I'll be your server today. Now, would you**
20   **prefer** *(Indicates opposite sides of the room)* **Clapping or**
21   **Non-Clapping section? And would you prefer Shaking or**
22   **Non-Shaking? Please be aware that if you sit in the Non-**
23   **Clapping section, then you cannot shake hands. So, if**
24   **you care to shake hands, you must sit in the Clapping**
25   **section. I'm sorry for any inconvenience, but that is the**
26   **new Code. We can't discriminate with our hands, now**
27   **can we? What's that? No, I'm sorry, if you're undecided,**
28   **you'll have to exit now. We seat those who are undecided**
29   **in the middle of the road.**

1 All right, you may take your seats. Just follow the usher
2 of your choice: Fred, in the orange coat, plaid pants, and
3 polka dot tie; Matt in all black with the Tazmanian Devil
4 tie — go get 'em, Taz! Or Butch in the chartreuse coat,
5 yellow tie, and gray gym shorts. He works with the youth.
6 As advertised, for those of you who are the first to sit right
7 down front, we are passing out these free *(Holds one up)*
8 automatic alarm watches. Now these *are* preset to alarm
9 at twelve o'clock, *(Substitute the time your service should*
10 *end)* twelve oh-two, oh-four, oh-six, oh-eight, and so forth.
11 If we have not finished serving you when the last one goes
12 off, you get a free personalized sermon delivered right to
13 your door.
14   Now, could I get your drink order? *(Pretends to be storing*
15 *the orders in her mind as she makes appropriate comments.)*
16 OK. All right! Uh-huh, got that. Oooo-kay. *(Rattles them off*
17 *rapidly, mumbling almost to herself the various drinks.)* **Tea,**
18 **coffee, water, decaf, Coke ...** *(Quickly)* **Sorry, we only have**
19 **grape juice and water.**
20   Would you like to hear about our specials today? We
21 have a prime solo. That is a filet of song laid on a bed of
22 soft piano music, seasoned with tone and modulation, and
23 brought to you on a red-hot microphone. We also have a
24 theme interpretation simmered in dramatic action,
25 seasoned with laughter, and that comes with applause on
26 the side.
27   While you're deciding, could I bring you an appetizer?
28 We have a prelude, a call to worship, a welcome, and a
29 prayer. Or I can bring a sample section of each for
30 everyone to share. While you're deciding, let me give you
31 your choices for music. We offer contemporary, classical,
32 hymns, praise bands, anthems, easy listening, gospel,
33 Christian rock, and oldies.
34   While you're deciding, I'll tell you that our breads today
35 are Matthew 4:4 and John 6:35. *(Or substitute the scripture*

1   *you will be using that day.)* **Our normal gratuity is ten**
2   **percent minimum, plus added amounts according to the**
3   **quality of your blessings. Our pastor du jour is** *(Name of*
4   *pastor)*, **and our sermon du jour is "Are You Serving or**
5   **Being Served?" We hope you'll enjoy our menu, but if not,**
6   **we trust you'll eat heartily anyway.**
7   **Well, I'll give you a few minutes to decide, and**
8   **someone will be here in a moment with your drinks.**

Cats Can See the Devil
by Tom X. Chao

1   *Tuesday, an idealistic, young, "up-and-coming" actress who*
2   *has only recently graduated from drama school, clutches her*
3   *glossy head shot as she speaks of her theatrical dreams to*
4   *Adrienne, a fellow struggling actress. At times eccentric and*
5   *neurotic, Tuesday frets about her career and wishes that she*
6   *could quickly carve her name in theatre history while serving*
7   *as a shining beacon to all the down-trodden and less fortunate.*
8
9   **TUESDAY:** *(Dreamily)* **I wish I was famous. Wouldn't that**
10 **be nice? I wish I didn't have to perform in tiny theatres**
11 **that nobody's ever heard of. I wish I could play the lead**
12 **role in a big show on Broadway. With my name up in**
13 **lights. I wish I could appear on TV and in movies and in**
14 **magazines. And everyone would know who I was. I'd be**
15 **so famous, people everywhere would recognize me.**
16 **Everywhere, all over the world.** *(Gradually more dramatic)* **I**
17 **wish I was so famous that even people in the most**
18 **remote locations on earth would be familiar with me. Even**
19 **in the most hellish, disease-ridden, war-stricken, famine-**
20 **ravaged, politically unstable countries, people would all**
21 **know me! Though they have no food to eat or water to**
22 **drink, they could draw spiritual and emotional sustenance**
23 **from the image of my face! My face! Shining down from**
24 **billboards and TVs and magazine covers! Bringing life to**
25 **the arid desert and frozen tundra! My face!** *(Pause.)*
26 **Well, you've got to have a dream.** *(Pause.)* **Oh, I know**
27 **it sounds egotistical. But you'd like to think that you**
28 **could rise above the level of —** *(She looks around, shrugs.)*
29 **You know.**

Pagan Babies
by Frank Mancino

1   *Sister Mary Magdalen is in a state of hypertension on*
2   *"Mission Day!" A tough-talking, wise-cracking, no-nonsense*
3   *nun who serves the Order of Obedience, Sister Mary knows*
4   *all and sees all. We catch a fleeting glimpse of her hard at*
5   *work in Latin class, soliciting donations from fearful students.*
6   *When she's funny, she's savagely funny. When she's serious,*
7   *she draws blood.*
8
9   **SISTER MARY:** OK, boys and girls, what day is it?
10 What? I can't hear you! That's right, it's ... Mission Day.
11 So, what are you waiting for? Lewandowski, you forget
12 your name or somethin'? You are first, whadda you got
13 for the Missions this morning? Ten cents? Good girl.
14 Next! Millinowich! Ten cents? God bless you, sweetie.
15 Next! Maruca! What? You don't have a dime today?
16 That's OK, Maruca, I will mark you down in the book for
17 twenty cents next week. Next! Naylor! Huh, you don't
18 have ten cents today, either? Hmmmm, lemme look ...
19 Says here you did not have your money last week,
20 either. *(Pause.)* Didn't I see you in the cafeteria
21 yesterday? Yes? And, didn't I see you eating an ice
22 cream cone? What flavor was it? Mint Chip, eh? *(Pause.)*
23 How much did that ice cream cone cost? Ten cents, eh?
24 So, are you telling me that you could not give up that
25 ice cream cone for the Missions, is that what you are
26 saying, eh? No, Naylor, your sister who sat in that exact
27 chair you sit in gave every week, and never failed. Never.
28 I was proud of her, a good Catholic girl, sat up straight,
29 kept her legs and mouth closed, and God willing, she

1   might join the Convent after college! She makes her
2   parents proud, I know. So, are you saying you don't want
3   to do as well as your sister, is that what you are saying?
4   No, of course not! Your parents would never stand for it.
5   So, Naylor, what are you going to do next time in the
6   cafeteria? You are going to give up any ice cream cone and
7   offer it up to the Missions? Ahhhh, I knew I could count on
8   you! OK, I will put you down in the book for thirty cents
9   next week, and if you don't have it all, we can loan you
10   some from the Bishop's fund, with interest, naturally.
11   Now, if you do that, I can let you bring in flowers and
12   make the first crown for Mary's Statue Crowning this
13   month. Would you like that? Good, just make sure they
14   are lilacs not roses, the thorns are not right for a May
15   crowning. OK, Go back to your desk now. Class, listen up!
16   Except for Naylor and Maruca, and some of the boys, I
17   must say that we are looking good. We are on track to win
18   the diocesan prize for the most Pagan Babies named, and
19   next week we will have enough to name our twenty-fifth
20   Pagan Baby this term. Now, think about a good Saint's
21   name for our Pagan Baby for next week.
22   OK, boys and girls, let's review your Latin before the
23   bell rings for the first period. So, first conjugation: *Amo,*
24   *Amas, Amat.* Repeat. *Amo, Amas, Amat.* Translation: I
25   love, you love, he/she loves. Repeat.

My Heart and the Real World
by Michael K. White

1   *An anxious, but not shy, romantic teenager slumps in an*
2   *armchair and dreams of the "Perfect Date." Her fantasy*
3   *voyage takes her to an idyllic wonderland filled with warm*
4   *embraces, heart-throbbing kisses, and electric-shock thrills.*
5   *The slow passage from dreary childhood to dreamy*
6   *adolescence is filled with a devotion and fidelity that reveals*
7   *the heart and soul of romantic love.*
8
9   **TEENAGER:** The perfect high school date would begin
10   in late afternoon with only a few hours before dark. The
11   boy would pick me up in his car and have Nine-Inch
12   Nails playing softly on his car stereo. As I got into the
13   car he would hand me a single white rose and,
14   laughingly, would say, "Good morning, how are you?"
15   While smiling and thanking him with a hug I would
16   notice that he was wearing his black leather pants and
17   that he had put on black eye liner. For that I would give
18   him a kiss on the cheek and he would begin to back out
19   of my driveway. He would then drive us out to a secret
20   place in the country with a couple of trees and an old,
21   abandoned camp ground. We would sit outside talking
22   and munching on food from a picnic basket until it got
23   dark. For the next couple of hours we would light
24   candles and watch the stars. I would get cold — on
25   purpose — and he would give me his jacket. When we
26   decided to leave we would pack everything up and go to
27   McDonald's by way of the drive-thru. He would tease me
28   about my "meatless Big Mac" as we drove to his house.
29   When there, we would sit in his living room and watch a

1 movie. I would fall asleep on his couch, and he would put
2 a blanket over me then finish watching the movie. When
3 the movie was over he would wake me to take me home
4 before my curfew. We would spend forever on my front
5 porch hugging each other good-bye because we didn't
6 want the night to end. Finally he would end this perfect
7 date with a shy kiss on my forehead and a "good night
8 sweetheart," and I would walk to my bedroom and fall
9 asleep with my head in the clouds.

Funnylogues for Women
by Mort Kaufman, Roger Karshner, and Zelda Abel

1   *Esther, a darkly serious and seasoned trouper from a long line*
2   *of show folks, has little patience with the artificial pretense of*
3   *the posturing "artiste." In accepting a creative artist award,*
4   *she takes a hard look at actors who hide from the truths they*
5   *discover in a series of smartly comic observations on the*
6   *acting profession. What she glimpses is amusing, but also*
7   *captures a deep wisdom that mixes theatre and life*
8   *experiences.*
9

10   **ESTHER:** We do two shows a day, and three on
11   Saturday. We work, really work. We just *do* it. We don't
12   stand around looking for motivation and attempt to be
13   artsy-fartsy. We're pros who get out there and knock
14   ourselves out and do our best to give people their
15   money's worth. And, sometimes, it isn't easy;
16   sometimes it's damned hard to get up for it because
17   you've done the show a million times. But, like I said —
18   we do it.
19   There are a lot of actors around who have deluded
20   themselves into believing they're this special package
21   set down on earth by divine grace, or something. That
22   their profession gives them an excuse to behave
23   strangely. Nonsense! Acting, the arts, all of it, is just
24   another profession, another choice. All of this
25   introspective, intellectual garbage about the "body" of
26   someone's work, for example, and about methods and
27   motivations is nothing but twenty tons of pure,
28   unadulterated nonsense spread in fifty directions.
29   You show me an artist who takes himself seriously,

and I'll show you stilted work and a person who has a nutritionist, changes religion once a week, breaks for sunbeams, and who, generally, has his Zen head up his yin-yang. Me, my family, we're troupers. We get out there and bust our buns to give people what they've paid their admission for — entertainment. We're entertainers.

And now we win this award and all of a sudden we discover we're "creative artists." And, well, I guess we are that, come to think of it. We're very much aware of "creating" a decent, enjoyable performance and "creating" a decent paycheck. One reviewer recently said this about us: "They are sensitive purveyors of the thespian art." With all due respect, I may be sick.

Changing Attire
by Robert Koon

1   *Barbara, a lonely waitress recovering from a painful breakup,*
2   *hurriedly gets dressed for a blind date as she chatters to her*
3   *roommate, a flight attendant. Suspecting that her roommate*
4   *does not adequately appreciate the gravity of this fragile*
5   *moment, Barbara offers a dark glimpse of the sad truth that*
6   *lurks beneath the surface of her frustration and failed hopes.*
7

8   BARBARA: You don't know how lucky you are. You
9   don't have to spend all this time thinking of what to
10   wear. You have uniforms. You're lucky.
11   But you know what's even luckier? When you guys
12   serve your meals, there are only entrees. Only two! Beef
13   or chicken. God, that must be so wonderful. I am so
14   sick and tired of people changing their order. Everybody
15   changes their order. You go back to the kitchen, give
16   them the order and then as soon as you get back out,
17   they call you over "Oh, miss." And it's not like you don't
18   have other people to take care of, but then you have to
19   go back in the kitchen, and they're all snooty about it,
20   too, and all you can say is "Hey, it's not my fault," but
21   they look at you like you're out there just making things
22   up, and you're not, and you'd think that, my god,
23   they've got the menu right in front of them, how hard
24   can it be to pick something and stay with it?
25   And another thing. This leaving the money on the
26   table and just walking out. What's up with that? I hate
27   that. Throw a couple of bills down and walk out. You go
28   over there and it's like, "I hope they left the right
29   amount. I hope they didn't just throw down a couple of

1   ones, just to look like they paid. I hope I don't have to go
2   chasing them down the street or anything." I mean, what
3   would it hurt to wait one minute and hand me the money
4   in person? What is this, anyway, "Hey, baby, give me what
5   I want and I'll leave the money on the table?" I mean, what
6   do I look like, a food prostitute?

Athena, Live!
by Danielle Dresden

1 *Murder, infidelity, and intrigue! Is it classical Greek tragedy or*
2 *daytime soap opera? It is both in* Athena, Live! *Loosely based*
3 *on Aeschylus'* Oresteia *trilogy — Iphigenia, daughter of*
4 *Agamemnon, is sacrificed by her father to gain fair winds for*
5 *the Greek ships bound for Troy — this is a re-telling of the*
6 *mythical tale in the format of a television talk show, with*
7 *Athena as the host. We now go to a live satellite hook-up from*
8 *an undisclosed witness protection program for an exclusive*
9 *interview with Iphigenia, who enters crisply wrapped in a*
10 *heavy cloak to tell her side of the story.*
11
12 **IPHIGENIA: Can you hear me, Athena?** *(She pauses and*
13 *seems to "hear" a go-ahead.)* **Sure, well, I'm Iphigenia,**
14 **daughter of Clytemnestra and Agamemnon. I'm in hiding**
15 **because I'm supposed to be dead. Only a miracle saved**
16 **me.**
17   **I guess it all started when my Uncle Menelaus married**
18 **my Aunt Helen, which surprised everybody because Helen**
19 **was so beautiful she could have had anybody in the world,**
20 **and Menelaus was at least a couple dishes short of a**
21 **complete table setting. Then Aunt Helen ran off with this**
22 **man, Paris, and Uncle Menelaus and my father**
23 **Agamemnon went nuts. They planned a hostile takeover**
24 **to get her back and destroy Paris and his organization, the**
25 **Trojans. I guess you can figure out what their business**
26 **was.**
27   **Anyway, my uncle and my father got so crazy they**
28 **wanted people blown away, and they made a deal with**
29 **these drug lords to be the wind. I'm not gonna say any**

1   more. No place is safe, you know what I mean? But the
2   tough guys wouldn't do anything unless Agamemnon made
3   a special voodoo pact with them to prove his loyalty. But
4   even my father balked at what they wanted him to do.
5   Everything came to a crashing halt. The hot-shot takeover
6   guys were going crazy. Finally, Agamemnon agreed.
7   Only my mother Clytemnestra and I didn't know about
8   any of this. All we knew is that suddenly we got a call from
9   Agamemnon saying he needs me to go help him. And it was
10 the most wonderful thing I could imagine. My father had ...
11 never said he needed me before. Not only that, I thought one
12 of his, I don't know, attorneys or lieutenants or whatever,
13 Achilles, was really cute, and I had a major crush on him. I
14 couldn't think of anything better. What a wonderful
15 adventure, you know, like finally I would mean something to
16 somebody. Maybe even two people. I dropped everything and
17 rushed off to Aulis.
18   When I got there it was so weird. Beyond weird. Strange.
19 Still. All these men were sitting or standing around, and their
20 eyes looked like BBs or something. Metallic. When I think
21 back, I swear I can hear drums, although I don't know if any
22 were really there. I see Achilles, and he's really cute, but he
23 looks sick, and I remember wondering if it's OK to drink the
24 water. It's like a jungle. The trees have big, broad, thick
25 leaves and there's sand everywhere and chickens. My father
26 looks like he's got a fever. Somebody's talking, about death,
27 honor and ... sacrifice. I wonder if they're going to kill a
28 chicken or something. Suddenly everyone looks at me. All
29 those dozens of pairs of flat, black, metallic eyes are looking
30 at me. It doesn't make any sense, but I know I'm the
31 sacrifice. So they're gonna do it. Kill me. *(Beat.)*
32   "Daddy?" I say. And as far as the world knows, I died. I
33 just wish I could have told my mother I didn't, 'cause maybe
34 she wouldn't have ...
35   I better break the connection now.

Chapter 4
Cracked Mirrors: Dark and Distorted

"These are weighty secrets ...
and we must whisper them."
— Sarah Chauncey Woolsey, *Secrets*

These fascinating but frail characters from full-length playscripts find themselves slipping deeper into dark despair that is mirrored in stark misfortune. Each shares a weighty secret and is forced to find a new way to rekindle the light within oneself. Some of the characters question if there is any point in pulling their lives together, while others reluctantly reach out to make new connections. All are searching for a truthful torch that will light the way out of the abyss of fractured dreams and frustrated hopes.

At first glance this is an exquisite portrait gallery of scheming rogues, broken victims, life's ideal spectators, hapless hostages, and eccentrics. Upon closer examination, however, it is evident that these finely etched characters are independent, resourceful, and — against all odds — unwilling to simply run away from their failures in life. While still shackled to traumatic events of the past, they have an unwavering optimism that softens an otherwise pained existence.

Unfortunately, no one character escapes unscathed — the damage has already been done. As you listen to the whispers of these characters, remember that there are perils to unearthing long buried secrets or discarded dreams. Think of these personal confessions as chronicles that draw comparisons between what *is* and what *was*. Do not discount each character's attempt to give insignificant events in their everyday life a sense of dignity or a small measure of self-worth. Although there is an abundance of gentle humor here, these stories are almost always tinged with an attempt to recapture the spirit of the past. The playwrights offer you bold new themes and deal with sensitive topics that capture the frustrating sense of life as we all know it ... and live it each day.

In playing the character roles of the dark and distorted, you will need to "personalize" the action without becoming overwhelmed by emotional intensity. Pay special attention to the atmosphere described in the monologues to better understand the emotional or psychological attitude that results in a specific character's mannerism or point of view. If your analysis blueprint has revealed repetitive character gestures or behavior patterns, these habitual actions may provide inventive performance opportunities for stage business or movement. A good starting point to consider is to voice the monologues in a more conversational tone to suggest intimacy or quiet urgency as the characters share their secrets aloud — perhaps for the first time. Although there may be moments of raging anger, refrain from inarticulate groans or grunts to indicate nonverbal responses or reactions. Don't forget to practice economy in the subtle use of facial expressions to indicate the private and personal nature of each character's solitary story.

Runaway Home
by Darren J. Butler

1   *At the tender age of thirteen, Aleah's childish innocence and*
2   *trust was shattered at the hands of her mother. For the last few*
3   *years she has lived with the haunting memory of a sexual*
4   *encounter with Harold, her mother's salesman boyfriend. The*
5   *traumatic event catapulted Aleah into a darker world of*
6   *depression, and here she describes the horrifying incident while*
7   *reliving her mother's disturbing decision.*
8

9   ALEAH: I grew up in a trailer park. We were the poorest
10   of poor. My daddy left me and my mom when I was about
11   three. Mom worked at a factory in the day and at a diner
12   in a truck stop at night. Even with both jobs, we were
13   barely making ends meet. Mom was one of those kind that
14   liked to spend her money on everything but the bills.
15   *(A tear rolls down her cheek.)* So, anyway, she met this
16   guy — Harold. He was one of her regular customers at the
17   diner. He was a salesman. They started seeing each other
18   and all. Well, the bill stuff got really bad, and they were
19   about to take our trailer and stuff ... so ... Harold told
20   mom that he would give her the money to get us totally
21   out of debt ... if he could ... have me ... a night with me.
22   *(Her voice becomes rigid and hateful.)* Mom took me
23   aside one afternoon before she went to work at the diner
24   and told me that Harold wanted to spend some time with
25   me, and that was cool with me ... I kind of liked him. I was
26   just glad she was happy and all. But then, she said that
27   she was gonna be gone all night and Harold was going to
28   stay with me. I thought this was strange, 'cause she never
29   worked all night at the diner. So I asked her if she was

1   working and she said no. So, I asked her where she was
2   going and she just said out, so that Harold could spend
3   the night with me. Then, she explained that he was gonna
4   pay off all our bills if I would stay the night with him.

5   *(Breaking down)* I was just numb. I didn't know what
6   to say. My own mother sold me to her boyfriend to pay our
7   bills. She got up and left for work, and Harold showed up
8   a little later. I was sitting on my bed when he came in the
9   room. He sat down beside me ... put his arm around me
10   ... and asked if my mom had explained things to me. I just
11   nodded. I had this lump in my throat, and I couldn't talk
12   or make a sound even if I wanted to. He started kissing
13   me and ...

14   *(She cries and tries to regain her composure.)* The next
15   morning Harold was gone, and there was this big wad of
16   cash on the kitchen table. I stared at it for the longest time
17   and then I went to my room, got everything I could stuff
18   into my backpack, grabbed that cash, and I never looked
19   back. *(In control)* I haven't seen or spoken to her since that
20   afternoon ... the day that she sold me.

Bridewell
by Charles Evered

1 *Kristen, an insecure young college student obsessed with her*
2 *weight, sits in the living room of her sorority house and*
3 *commiserates with her "sisters" about men and their unfailing*
4 *ways. She tries to console her friend Amanda's broken heart by*
5 *explaining how she copes with the demon love. But the*
6 *comforting story only provides more insight and unanswered*
7 *questions about Kristen herself.*
8
9 KRISTEN: Look, just be glad you're not me. If you were
10 me you'd be on your second box of Twinkies by now. I love
11 food at a time like this. I wish I could eat for you now.
12 Come to think of it, I probably will later. I remember when
13 ... I can't say the name ... but when "a certain someone"
14 *ripped my heart out.* It was my total low point. I was going
15 to those Overeaters Anonymous meetings with my mother
16 — which is kind of ironic, because she's the person who
17 used to shove food in my face all the time anyway. So, this
18 "certain someone" *dumps* me, and as my mother is
19 driving us home it's like, what do ya know, she just
20 happens to stop at a Rite-Aid and out she comes with a
21 ten-pound box of candy, and all I remember after that was
22 seeing our twenty pudgy little fingers pulling and twisting
23 and gouging out the candies and me just shoving them
24 into my mouth, and that's when I got this great idea. "I
25 won't eat them," I thought. I'll just chew them. If I chew
26 them without swallowing, then I never will have eaten
27 them at all. And all of this will have been nothing but a
28 bad dream. So I put like fourteen of them in my mouth
29 and I just chomped, but without swallowing, feeling all the

1   chocolaty juices sliding down my throat and my brain
2   flooding with endorphins, and after about eight minutes I
3   hacked out this huge ball of nougat and caramel and deftly
4   wrapped it up in a napkin and calmly put it on the
5   dashboard and repeated the process over and over until all
6   the candy was gone. So, I'm sitting there, candy wrappers
7   all over me and sweat pouring down my forehead, and my
8   mom turns to me and says, "Ya know what Pudgy-Poo, we
9   can freeze those hacked up balls. No use wasting good
10   candy."

Dead

by Mort Kaufman, Roger Karshner, and Zelda Abel

1 *Although this unidentified woman may view life as just one,*
2 *long continuous gag, she thinks aloud about those other*
3 *woebegone folks who have a weird fascination with funerals.*
4 *She recites her sardonic point about the outrageous ritual of*
5 *death and dying with a deadpan delivery and a blistering,*
6 *outrageously funny inventory of popular customs and fads.*
7

8 WOMAN: What's with people who love funerals? It's like
9 they just can't get enough of the dead. They love
10 visitations. "Don't mind me, I'm just hanging around
11 enjoying the body." In fact, I think they like dead people
12 better than live people. Well ... come to think of it ... I
13 mean ... dead people don't talk back, they're quiet,
14 respectful, they don't interrupt, they don't lie, they don't
15 steal, they're clean, always dressed nice, they never show
16 up at your house unexpected when you're sitting around
17 trimming your toenails. Hey, come to think of it, dead
18 people are damned near perfect.
19   Why is it that their hands are always folded over their
20 chests? What if they'd been in the military? Wouldn't it be
21 more realistic if they were saluting? *(Salutes.)* Or if they'd
22 been politicians? *(Waves.)* Or impatient drivers ... ? *(Makes*
23 *a rude gesture.)*
24   Have you ever noticed how people talk to the corpse?
25 Say stuff like, "Well, take it easy now, Jane." How easy
26 can you take it? Look ... if dead isn't easy, I'm not going.
27 Or, "Well, now you'll be with your friends." What if they
28 didn't have any friends? Like my uncle, Leonard, who was
29 universally hated by everybody. Of course, when he died

he was "a wonderful person," "wouldn't hurt a fly," "everybody loved him," "he'll be missed." How the hell could he be missed? Nobody would have anything to do with him. But now that he's dead he was sweet, wonderful, kind ... generous. Generous. I guess alluva sudden everyone forgets about the time he got caught taking money out of the March of Dimes display. But now he's dead, now he's perfect, now he's going to join Aunt Rose, who divorced him for exposing himself to her Meals on Wheels woman.

Then there are the remarks about how good the body looks. You were sick for over a year, you lost your hair and fifty pounds, but now you're fabulous. "Doesn't he look good?" "Isn't she beautiful?" "She never looked lovelier." When you're alive all you hear is how rotten you look. "You don't look so good." "Have you been getting enough sleep?" "If I were you, and I don't mean to alarm you, but I'd see a doctor." When you're alive nobody ever says you look good. But die and it's, "Doesn't he look great?" "Isn't she beautiful?" Their whole lives people are saving up compliments for when you're dead.

What Is Gained
by Evan Guilford-Blake

1   *Ms. Grinch, a high-strung young woman who stutters when*
2   *talking excitedly, is nearly at the end of her tinsel rope! It's the*
3   *yuletide season again, and her mood changes swiftly from*
4   *denial to despair in keeping with the holiday spirit. Haunted by*
5   *childhood memories of her shiny new red fire truck squashed*
6   *by a runaway dump truck, Ms. Grinch has never been able to*
7   *replace her lost fire truck ... or reclaim her lost youth.*
8
9   **MS. GRINCH:** *You* **dare ask me: Why am I like this?** *Why?*
10   **All right, Donald. I'll tell you!** *Because* **...**
11   **of — Christmas!**
12   **When I was eleven, I got the** *best* **Christmas present in**
13   **the world! A bright red fire truck — just like my daddy**
14   **rode on. And I went outside right away, and I was**
15   **vrooming with my new truck, up and down the**
16   **driveway —**
17   *(She acts it out.)* **Vroom, vroooommmm ... And I was**
18   **having so much ffff— ffff— ffff— fun — just going back**
19   **and forth, up and down. It was a beautiful Christmas day,**
20   **very warm, the sun was bright and there wasn't a cloud for**
21   **miles. And there I was with my shiny new red truck, just**
22   **— vroooommmm, vroooommmm, vroooommmm ... I let it**
23   **go, and it** *ran,* **fast, faster, faster, like a racecar, down the**
24   **driveway and into the —** *(She starts to get sadder)* **street,**
25   **and this big dump truck was coming along and I didn't see**
26   **it and it — ran over my shiny new red fire truck and —**
27   ***squashed* it — flat as a ten-year-old's chest. I took it back**
28   **into the house and showed it to my mother and father, but**
29   **they said we couldn't afford to replace it and that I'd have**

1   to wait till next year for Santa to bring me one. And I was
2   a good girl, all year. I cleaned my room and I brushed my
3   teeth and I even ate my stinkin' broccoli, and then I wrote
4   Santa a letter asking for just two things, a bicycle and a
5   new fire truck. I *got* the bicycle, but ... but the truck never
6   came, not that year, not ever. And I really, really, *really*
7   wanted the truck, more than anything else in the whole
8   world. And so I — stopped sending letters, and being nice
9   and having ffff— ffff— ffff— *fun* — and I wanted to make
10   a lot of money so I could buy all the trucks I wanted; but
11   I could never find another one *just* like the one daddy rode
12   on ...
13   So, now I'm _____ *(Indicate age)*, and you and the whole
14   damn world think I'm Mrs. Grinch. Well, too bad! I'm
15   not — I'm *Ms.* Grinch to you, and if you don't like it you
16   can take a long vroom off a short driveway yourself!

Happy Endings
by Judith Hancock

1 *It is New Year's Eve in the Big Apple, glittering New York City,*
2 *as a small group of intimate chums gathers for a boisterous*
3 *celebration but instead passes the time sharing fond childhood*
4 *memories. Marcella, a shy and reserved young woman, stuns*
5 *her friends when she reveals a "dirty little secret" about an age*
6 *of innocence that was not that innocent after all.*
7
8 MARCELLA: My father was a peeping Tom.
9 Don't look at me like that, Bobbye! I can't talk about it if
10 you look at me.
11   He only did it when I took a shower.
12   I'd hear this small squeak and then the bathroom door
13 would open a crack.
14   *(Marcella puts two fingers up, almost touching.)* A small
15 crack — like a peep. *(Beat.)*
16   The first time it happened, I thought it was one of my
17 brothers. I even flounced around a little, like it was a
18 game. *(Beat.)*
19   Then I realized who it was ... *(Beat.)*
20   He never did anything. He'd just look at me through
21 that slit in the door. You know how it was, Bobbye. *(Beat.)*
22   That crowded Bronx apartment with all the double-
23 decker beds and there was only one bathroom with a lock
24 that never worked. I'd shower early — it was the only time
25 I knew the bathroom was free. My mother slept half of the
26 day, and you'd have to scream to wake up my brothers.
27   *(Beat.)* I felt like I was frozen when he looked at me —
28 like the shower water was ice, like I was locked inside this
29 huge, thick ice house ... and no one would ever come to

1   **carve me out ...** *(Marcella shivers.)*
2   **I never told anyone.** *(Beat.)*
3   **That was part of it, not telling.** *(Beat.)*
4   **It was our dirty little secret.**

Bones
by Kerri Kochanski

1 *Genny, a dark-edged young woman who feels she is*
2 *suffocating in her own body, stands quietly center stage with*
3 *the sleeves of her oversized sweater pulled tightly over her*
4 *hands. Although she is painfully thin, Genny can no longer see*
5 *the bones in her ribcage and imagines she is not as thin as she*
6 *could be — or should be. In this riveting outcry she appears to*
7 *be on the verge of drowning in her own despair, pulled down*
8 *by the undertow of self-denial.*
9

10 GENNY: *Food* sticks ... When you are washing it down
11 with milkshakes, food sticks ... It sticks to your *ribs* ...
12 And your *hip* bones ... I never thought that I *had* a hip
13 bone ...
14 *(She remembers, afraid.)* But one time I was *very* sick.
15 *Very* sick — and I saw ...
16 *(Quietly)* ... a hip bone ...
17 *(Looks at audience, pointedly.)* And a rib ...
18 Ribs that were so *pronounced* ...
19 *(Quietly)* ... that it made my father cry ...
20 *(Deepening)* It made *me* cry ...
21 *(Deeper, darker)* To see my father, crying ...
22 *(Resuming)* Because he never did cry, you know. Even
23 during the worst times.
24 Times when — I don't know. He lost some money in
25 the stock market.
26 Or when his mother died. He didn't even cry when his
27 *mother* died.
28 *(Remembers.)* But when he saw me ...
29 *(Trails off, sadly. Beat.)* Ribs ... Sticking to ribs ... The

1   food sticks ...

2   Usually you can't see the ribs. When you eat.

3   When you eat things like nuts and milkshakes —

4   *(Protesting, scared)* Things I don't *want* to eat but I have

5   no ...

6   Stuff I don't *want* to — Force inside ...

7   *(Growing scared)* I don't want to force ...

8   But he's feeding me. My dad is feeding me ...

9   *(She begins to become very disturbed.)* I *can't* eat it ... I

10   don't *want* to *eat* it ...

11   *(Pointing to her ribs, through tears.)* It *sticks* inside of

12   me ... It sticks to my *ribs* ...

13   *(She lifts up her sweater, showing her torso. Crazily)* You

14   *see*? You *see*?

15   *(She pokes at her ribcage.)* You *can't* see it ... You can't

16   see *ribs* ...

17   *(She is upset. She brings her sweater down, and tucks it*

18   *into her pants, not wanting anyone to see. She hugs her arms*

19   *around herself, sadly.)*

Bedside Manners
by Lisa Stephenson

1   *Chris, an opinionated, high-profile wedding consultant with a*
2   *quick wit, relaxes in her room at a quaint New England bed-*
3   *and-breakfast. She revels in her ongoing success of parading*
4   *brides up and down the aisle. Here she reminisces about some*
5   *of the unspeakable lessons learned from her festive wedding*
6   *celebrations, and offers some memorable snapshots of her*
7   *celebrity clients.*
8

9   CHRIS: I keep telling myself that this is not life or death.
10   I keep telling my clients that it's not life or death. I try to
11   soothe their nerves and calm their anxiety. But I'm a
12   wedding consultant. Not Sigmund Freud. People may look
13   normal, but just mention the word wedding and you can
14   fill a padded cell with inmates who buy Valium in the giant
15   economy size.

16   I just got back from helping another satisfied
17   customer. A repeat business bride who's married husband
18   number three. She claims I help keep her sanity. I wish I
19   could help her keep a husband. My job is like doing
20   penance for Lent three-hundred sixty-five days a year.
21   When I meet Saint Peter at the gates, I want him to be
22   dressed in any color but white.

23   When I started in the business I thought tulle was a
24   hammer. Then I learned the differences. Not only between
25   chiffon and organza, but between women and brides.
26   Females start as the first and become the second. The
27   metamorphosis is not always pretty.

28   I had one bride who tried on dresses for six and a half
29   hours. When she finally said, "Wrap it up," the whole

bridal department at Saks and two security guards burst
into applause. One of my favorites was a mail-order match
made in heaven. The bride was Russian and was anxious
to embrace the land of the free, the home of the brave, and
the alterations department at Kleinfeld's. I also planned a
ceremony for two men who wanted to publicly affirm and
declare their love. It wasn't easy finding white peau de soie
pumps, size fourteen.

Last year I did a Hollywood wedding — eight hundred
guests and the bride in a fantasy gown. It combined the
best design concepts of Good Witch Glinda and the
Chrysler Building. California people like things that float in
pools — gardenias, lilies, and guests. The wedding was
beautiful, but different. Like people in California.

I help with everything. I'm their friend, confidant, and
budget advisor. If I did any more I could double my fee and
be their shrink. When you consider the possibilities of
guaranteed employment — babies, weddings, and funerals
— or, as we say in the trade, hatches, matches, and
dispatches — I'm glad I've chosen the one that sees
people happy. Women thinking they're beautiful and
parents sighing with relief.

I, myself, have never been married. What holds me
back? It's the part of the vows, "Till death do us part." I've
never wanted to participate in something that might make
me consider murder or suicide.

Cleveland Raining
by Sung Rno

1 *Mari, an intelligent and sensitive Korean-American medical student*
2 *who sees herself as a "healer," lives with her older brother, Jimmy,*
3 *a failed artist. Abandoned by her mother as a small child, Mari is now*
4 *distraught about the mysterious disappearance of her father, who has*
5 *been missing nearly a week. She sits on the front porch staring at a*
6 *medical book, but puts it away to read from her diary and relives the*
7 *puzzling dream she had the past night.*
8
9 MARI: This was my dream last night. I'm driving down the
10 interstate and it's overcast. I can see the highway stretching
11 over the plains for miles, but I look to my right and see a farm,
12 cows grazing, but past all of this I see trees stretched out
13 across the sky, the stalks of wheat are like porridge, like hair,
14 like someone's belly, and then it seems like I can see even
15 further, that past the fields, past the farms, I see ... water ...
16 and waves, and I can smell the salt, the heat, the taste of that
17 sea.
18   I feel like turning the car into that wetness, that abyss. Only
19 there's the shoulder, there's the guardrail, so I ignore it, I keep
20 driving, I keep my eyes on the road. But I can't stop looking over
21 there, into that invisible lake in the side of my vision, so finally
22 ... I do it ... I turn, I take a sharp turn, I'm turning and —
23   Then I'm flipping ... through the air ... flying and flipping ...
24 over the barrier, up and over, there's the totally pure moment
25 of silence, and then it's all noise: concrete, glass, the car, the
26 air, the metal breaking, all of it breaking, and I'm bleeding, I'm
27 in pain, I'm hurt, but I can't tell you, I can't tell you how happy
28 I feel.

Epiphany Cake
by Kelly Younger

1   *Alice, a sophisticated "New York, New York" African American*
2   *novelist, is sent by her agent to an all-white, all-female book*
3   *reading group in suburban Los Angeles. It isn't long before she*
4   *discovers that every one of the women in the group has lied*
5   *about reading her novel of the slave girl, Daphne, making her*
6   *way to America. After an awkward confrontation, a defiant*
7   *Alice reveals a secret of her own.*
8
9   **ALICE: Mainstream America is white. And if you want a**
10   **best-seller, you better write to a white audience. And white**
11   **America doesn't want to read a story about some black**
12   **girl dating their white son, and some black girl coming to**
13   **dine at the country club, and some black girl making**
14   **something of herself on her own. If it's that kind of story,**
15   **America needs some distance. Set it a hundred years ago,**
16   **they said. Make Daphne a slave, they said. Write about the**
17   **Middle Passage, and plantations, and the Civil War, Mr.**
18   **Lincoln, and, oh yes, throw in the occasional "yes massah,**
19   **yes massah," and the readers will eat it up. You'll get every**
20   **book club stamp from Oprah to *The Today Show* and then**
21   **some. Housewives all across the nation will discuss your**
22   **book over wine and cheese, or in your case, cake. And who**
23   **cares if they get it or not, they bought it, and that's money**
24   **in your pockets. America doesn't care why the caged bird**
25   **sings or what color purple is. All they care about is**
26   **relieving their guilt over the past. And my, oh my, isn't it**
27   **easier to read a book about black people than to actually**
28   **talk to some?**

Cocktail Hour at Gibson Southern High School's Tenth Year Reunion
by Elizabeth Dembrowsky

1   *Brenda Pinto, thin, gorgeous, successful, and rich, returns to her*
2   *old hometown for the first time in ten years to attend a class*
3   *reunion at Gibson Southern High School. Although ambivalent*
4   *about her former classmates and their attitudes toward her*
5   *success, Brenda agrees to address the full group. She only*
6   *speaks one-half of what she is actually thinking — the other*
7   *half is spoken under her breath and indicated in italics.*
8
9   **BRENDA:** *Oh, God, I absolutely hate these things.*
10 *(Smiles.)*
11   **How nice to see you!** *I cannot believe I have to be at*
12 *one of these with you people.*
13   **Oh, no, it's my pleasure, anytime** ... *My agent better*
14 *never do this to me again.*
15   **I absolutely adore these things.** *Compared to root*
16 *canals.*
17   **So nice to see old friends again, things haven't**
18 **changed a bit** ... *Except the number of husbands you've*
19 *divorced and facelifts you have had.*
20   **You haven't aged a day.** *But those ten years really*
21 *make you look like you've lived through twenty.*
22   **I love what you've done with your hair.** *And how it*
23 *hides most of your face.*
24   **Oh, this old thing — awwww, stop, it's nothing.** *But*
25 *compared to the burlap bags you folks are wearing, of*
26 *course it must look nice.*
27   **A speech from me? Oh, no, I couldn't.**
28   *(She walks center stage and stands in front of an invisible*
29 *podium. Straightens invisible microphone and begins.)* **When I**

1   was first invited here to speak, I was in shock *that anyone*

2   *would think I would want to come back here.*

3   It is an honor and a privilege *for you to be able to hear*

4   *me speak.*

5   And I thank you *for the open bar that you've provided.*

6   Ten years ago when I left the hallowed halls of Gibson

7   Southern High School, *I ran.*

8   *Far away.*

9   I never dreamed that I would be here again. *I had*

10   *nightmares, plenty of nightmares.*

11   Standing before you, my fellow class of ninety-six-ers,

12   *Thin, gorgeous, successful and rich,*

13   I have so many memories from my high school days.

14   *None of them good.*

15   And I will never forget them. *No matter how much*

16   *therapy I go through.*

17   I thank you from the bottom of my heart, *for making*

18   *me look so good.*

19   And I wish you all that you deserve.

It Doesn't Take a Tornado
by Rosanna Yamagiwa Alfaro

1 *A formidable but now dissolute woman sits slumped in front of*
2 *her mangled trailer home surrounded by debris and wreckage,*
3 *talking to a local television reporter and camera crew. What*
4 *appears to be a devastating disaster, however, is in plain fact a*
5 *comic blessing as the woman quietly explains how it took a*
6 *tornado to clean her house — and finally get rid of her ex-*
7 *husband!*
8
9 WOMAN: Do I have a minute to spare? Young lady, you
10 can have a minute, an hour ... you can have the rest of my
11 life, if you want it. I've already talked to the Fire Chief —
12 he's a nice man — and the Deputy Coroner — he's a real
13 jerk — and someone from the County Sheriff's Office.
14 Well, I guess I'm the only one left around here to talk to.
15 Everyone else is lying in the morgue or, worse yet, the city
16 hospital. It was awful! My dog, Hank? I saw him sailing
17 through the air, all seventy pounds of him. He just flew
18 past along with the two cats. Damn.
19   The trailer's OK. Thank God. The forest behind
20 me — untouched. Not a branch, not a twig fell to the
21 ground. You don't believe me? Go look for yourself.
22 Tornadoes are attracted to metal — that's why my trailer's
23 out of the loop, backed up against the forest. I was in my
24 bathtub with a mattress over my head, but all the time I
25 felt I'd come out of this just fine — which I did, thank
26 God.
27   Most everyone else, they lost all they had. Howie and
28 Janice in number two? They were headed for a divorce,
29 and this will speed things up, you betcha. That shiny

1   sixty-five-foot trailer that was trucked in here just
2   yesterday? When its owners come looking for it, they'll find
3   it on its side over there in the swamp. I sat out here and
4   watched the whole thing until it got too close. I tell you, it
5   was amazing. The smell of the electricity in the air, the
6   way that funnel touched down here, then there, taking our
7   power lines, boom! Kaboom! Then it sat right down on the
8   trailer park and wiped it off the face of the earth.
9   It's a sad business. My ex-husband in number six?
10 Roof fell in on top of him and broke his back. *(Beat.)* Oh,
11 don't be too sorry. I'm certainly not. Put him out of his
12 misery, poor slob. *(Beat.)* Children? Two of them. Molly's in
13 California. Matt, in Florida, I think. I tell you, it doesn't
14 take a high wind to scatter a family to the four corners of
15 the earth. It doesn't take a killer tornado. Other accidents
16 can throw you off course. *(Beat.)*
17   The day I kicked him out of my house it was like I was
18 ridding myself of this huge weight that was killing me. I
19 took everything of his I could find and threw it out after
20 him — his six packs, his stacks of *Hustler*, his armchair.
21 I tell you, it was like throwing boulders, uprooting trees,
22 and hurling them at him. Well, now it seems God's seen fit
23 to finish up my work. It takes a tornado to clean house.

Squats
by Martin Jones

1 *Cece, a sadly familiar homeless teenager, has holed up in a*
2 *cheap motel with Tucker, a much older and also homeless ex-*
3 *con. They have spent the night drinking and telling each other*
4 *stories about the misdeeds that led to their incarcerations. Here,*
5 *Cece recalls how she became an arsonist at an early age. She*
6 *remembers her youth with a mixture of bragging and a touch*
7 *of wistful sadness about her past. Cece's sobering experiences*
8 *offer a cynical critique of the lost and forlorn who try to find*
9 *order and meaning in the present by coming to terms with the*
10 *haunting specters of their past.*
11
12 **CECE:** *(Sighs heavily.)* **Well, I set my first [fire] when I was**
13 **about nine or ten. The summer my old man left us. Me**
14 **and Bobby Conroy ... we were playin' in his daddy's old**
15 **milk barn. This was when we still lived up at Rumford.**
16 **Anyway, we were punchin' holes in the barn wall with a**
17 **ball-peen hammer. Bobby found a can of paint thinner in**
18 **the tack room. And I supplied the matches. Went up like**
19 **the Fourth of July. All the neighborin' farmers stood on**
20 **the hill, watchin' it burn all night long. I was scared, so I**
21 **was hidin' behind my mama's legs, but I'd peek out from**
22 **time to time from behind her dress. She was cryin'. I think**
23 **she knew. She squeezed my hand so hard I got a big**
24 **bruise, but I didn't care. I couldn't take my eyes offa those**
25 **colors reachin' up to that black sky — all sorta Christmas**
26 **red and Florida orange. Bobby Conroy finally broke down**
27 **and confessed. Got his ass whipped good. I never told.**
28 **Mama didn't say nothin', but I could tell she knew.**
29 *(Pause.)* **Couple years later, she'd be at work at the paper**

1   mill — be gone all day — and I'd be home alone or in
2   school — always thinkin' about those colors. Couldn't get
3   'em outta my head. That summer, I sorta went wild. I
4   burnt three barns, an old fishin' boat, and a couple of
5   abandoned house trailers. Then I got caught ...
6   You think that's funny?
7   I never did it to hurt people. Just like to watch things
8   burn. I set some brush fires too. Some guy showed me
9   how. He'd catch a big ol' jack rabbit in a snare, then he'd
10   hold the rabbit by his ears, and dunk his hindquarters in a
11   bucket of kerosene. Light the tail, and set him loose. A
12   jackrabbit will zig-zag two or three miles 'fore he realizes
13   he's dead. I didn't do much of that, 'cause I didn't like the
14   idea of killin' anything, even if it was a pesky rabbit.

Anorexia
by Peter Langman

1   *Fran, a thin and pretty but distressed young girl in her late*
2   *teens, suffers from an obvious eating disorder. She is living in a*
3   *state of denial, on the brink of disaster. Fran offers a chilling*
4   *glimpse of the guessing game she plays with her life each day,*
5   *hopelessly addicted to hunger. This is a sober self-portrait of a*
6   *young girl's tortured efforts to come to terms with a disease that*
7   *has changed her life forever.*

8

9   **FRAN:** I don't know how I got this way. My life used to
10   seem so good. I had a nice home. My parents cared about
11   me. I wasn't abused or anything. But somehow, I never
12   knew what I needed. I always felt like I was above having
13   needs. At least, I tried to be. To need something or
14   someone was to be incomplete. I didn't want to be
15   incomplete. I wanted to be perfect. I didn't even recognize
16   that I had feelings. Aren't feelings a sign of weakness?
17   Even more, they are a sign of being a person. After all, I
18   wasn't anybody. Who was I to have feelings? I wasn't
19   worthy enough, and if I did feel something, I didn't allow
20   myself to recognize it. I didn't merit the right to my anger,
21   and, having to be perfect, wouldn't accept that I could be
22   angry, because anger was bad and I couldn't possibly be
23   bad.

24   I lived for praise. I had to be excellent in everything so
25   I would be praised and find approval, because inside, I was
26   nothing. Everything had to come from outside, because I
27   had nothing to give myself. And yet, I never wanted to rely
28   on others. I wanted to be strong, independent, self-
29   sufficient. But I was so empty, I was completely

1   dependent on what other people thought of me. So I was
2   nice to everyone, and never rocked the boat, never
3   expressed an opinion, never disagreed with anyone. I just
4   had to keep everyone happy with me.
5   It's like I was playing dead — I had no needs, I had no
6   feelings. People tried to talk to me, but it was like their
7   words were coming through a fog that blurred their sounds
8   so much I couldn't comprehend what they were saying. I
9   was so lost in my own world that their words couldn't
10   reach me.
11   It got to the point where even praise became
12   meaningless. All I wanted was to disappear. I began
13   exercising. I stopped eating. I dressed in loose clothes to
14   hide my body. But it didn't work. My relationship with my
15   body seems like such a private, personal thing to me, but
16   at the same time, it's all so horribly public, and people
17   think they have the right to comment on how I look and
18   what I'm doing to myself. Can't they just leave me alone?
19   It's not about them.
20   Starving is like a drug that makes you crazy. You can't
21   see straight. You can't think straight. The whole world
22   vanishes and is replaced by thoughts of food. I think of it
23   all the time. I even dream about it. I watch shows about
24   cooking food. I study the nutrition of food. I even prepare
25   food for others. I do everything with food — but eat it.

Chapter 5
Stained Mirrors:
Pain and Sorrow

"Life goes on forever ...
like the gnawing of a mouse."
— Edna St. Vincent Millay, *Ashes of Life*

These forlorn characters from full-length playscripts look into the stained mirror and see a reflection of pain and sorrow that takes their breath away. But they are brave souls, and unflinching in spite of the despair that hangs all around them. They bear the unbearable with a dignity that is surprising, and sometimes even darkly comic. Most of the characters are in a desperate search for self-affirmation, seeking a way to celebrate life — even if that celebration is only a dull reflection stained with tears.

The playwrights here are very pointed in their treatment of the more dissolute aspects of the human condition, where even innocent characters fall victim to circumstances over which they have no control. The larger truth revealed in these character depictions, however, is that we are all subject to slow, inevitable pain and sorrow — like the gnawing of a mouse.

In some instances, these are unsettling stories that strip away all pretense and call unwanted attention to the frailty of human life. In other instances, there are stories nothing less than an anthem to the indestructibility of the human spirit that still clings to a flickering glimpse of hope. In the end, however, it is clear that the dark forces in these character's lives are overpowering and will inevitably cast them back into the bleakness they have struggled to escape. As you read these personal testaments, look for the essential life spirit in each character. There you may discover how the darker side of human misery can also serve to sharpen our understanding of *who* we are, even if we are unable to rescue ourselves with that knowledge. Finally, look for those rare moments where the characters accept the crushing truth of life and embrace the pain and sorrow that inevitably follows.

In playing the character roles of pain and sorrow, rely on an analysis blueprint to outline the dominant personality traits and mannerisms that give added dimension to your portraits. Do not merely copy what you have discovered in analysis, or observed in the rehearsal period. To take that approach would result in a stale performance and would not accurately mirror the basic impulses of these characters. Focus, instead, on performance approaches that display the character's sense of humility and quiet dignity. Look for clues in the text that underline the deception and delusion that gives some of the characters a dark and corrosive self-image. You should also use this opportunity to reduce and refine these character portraits to performance metaphors in the rehearsal period to capture their individuality in attitude, action, and intention.

She Must Like It
by Tom Coash

1   *Ms. Smith, an educated and fiercely independent African*
2   *American woman, proclaims self-respect, pride, and identity as*
3   *essential qualities in combating racial stereotypes. Although*
4   *she finds herself living in the shadow of an abusive relationship*
5   *with a husband who drinks too much, Ms. Smith remains*
6   *headstrong and defiant in her convictions as she tries to*
7   *heroically navigate the rivers of racial bias.*
8

9   **MS. SMITH:** "I would never let that happen to me." "Why
10   doesn't she leave?" "She must like it." Man, I get tired of
11   hearing that. You wanna know why I didn't leave? 'Cause
12   I was determined not to fall into that white folks
13   stereotype of "Mama on welfare and a bunch of fatherless,
14   delinquent kids." I took the violence for years to avoid
15   being that welfare mother white folks hated, only to have
16   them turn around and tell me that I should have left long
17   ago and applied for welfare.
18   I'm a strong woman. A college graduate. Had a nice
19   home, a respectable job, and a husband who worked. Now
20   am I mistaken or isn't that the American Dream? Now, am
21   I gonna give up all that and go on welfare with my three
22   kids, become the white man's burden, because my
23   husband drinks too much Colt Forty-Five one night and
24   shoves me? Or slaps me? Think about it. I got pride. I'm
25   stubborn. I talked to my pastor 'bout it, 'bout the abuse
26   he was putting me through. And pastor told me I need to
27   turn the other cheek, that it was my cross to bear. Think
28   of the family. Children need their father. Finally "their
29   father" started beating on my oldest and I had him

1   arrested. I went to court and I tried to explain to this judge
2   that I wanted him punished so he knows it was serious but
3   not so's he lose his job. 'Cause then we'd just have
4   another black man out on the street, plus we needed his
5   support money. And the judge said I was wasting the
6   court's time and did I want him in jail or not? All the time
7   my husband is saying he didn't do anything. So I finally
8   said, "OK, put him away for the rest of his life, I don't
9   care." Then the man says, "Now, come on, he is your
10 husband after all." Finally, I just said the hell with it. They
11 give him probation.
12   First thing he came home, he hit me with his fist
13 'cause I guess he figured he can get away with it now. And
14 I hit him back 'cause that's what I told myself I would do.
15 Well he hit me again ... hard ... and that ... that was a real
16 wake up call. I called the cops. He said I hit him first. They
17 arrested us both. Uh hunh, that's right. Like I hurt him.
18 Like I'm the batterer. I mean, he's never been afraid of me.
19 He doesn't have to pay attention to what kind of mood I'm
20 in when I come in from work. He doesn't have to watch
21 everything he says when we're at a party because he's
22 afraid I'll beat hell out of him when we get home. It
23 seemed like everywhere I turned in this thing I got police,
24 social worker, lawyer, judge, and God, all wanting to tell
25 me my business. You know who's the only real expert on
26 this thing? Me! And when I talked ... nobody listened.

Big Girl
by Andrew Biss

1   *Peggy, a "big girl" with an acerbic sense of humor, shares*
2   *childhood memories of her Aunt Nester, who died suddenly*
3   *after suffering a severe stroke while pruning her beloved*
4   *roses. Along the way, Peggy shares thoughts on the subject*
5   *of self-image that are serious stuff to be sure, and provides a*
6   *fleeting glance at the sort of prejudice we are all familiar with*
7   *— our own!*
8

9   PEGGY: I've always been big. I was born big. I was a big
10 baby. Still am in some respects. In fact, one of the
11 earliest memories I have is of my Aunt Nester staring
12 down at me, her thin lips contorted into a forced
13 expression of adoration, saying to my mother, "My
14 word, you've got a big girl there, haven't you, Georgie?"
15 *(Beat.)* She's dead now. Not my mother — my Aunt
16 Nester. A severe stroke while pruning her beloved roses
17 in her front garden. She fell into them face first, the
18 thorns of her pride and joy gashing open her wizened
19 face in her moment of need. They did a good job,
20 though — at the mortuary, that is. She looked quite
21 regal, all dished up and served before us, there in her
22 casket. I stared hard at her face, but I couldn't see even
23 the trace of a scar. Mum fell apart. Sadly, all I felt was
24 a slight twinge of guilt as I contorted my not-so-thin lips
25 into a forced expression of loss.
26   *(Beat.)* And so it goes.
27   *(Pause.)* I think self-hatred is vastly underrated, don't
28 you? I mean, everyone seems to have such a negative
29 view of it. But if you really think about it, it makes life

1   so much easier in so many ways. For a start, you don't
2   have to bother giving yourself all those tiresome
3   confidence-building pep talks inside your head every time
4   you look in the mirror or step outside the front door. You
5   can simply hate what you see before you, shrug your
6   shoulders, and get on with your business. And if someone
7   insults you or shoots you a disdainful glare, it doesn't
8   sting or chip away at your delicately crafted shell of self-
9   confidence — it just lands harmlessly in that boggy pit of
10   everything you already despise anyway, and fizzles out
11   with barely a flicker. You don't wrestle with it, you just
12   absorb it. It can save an awful lot of time in this fast-paced
13   world of ours. Think about it.
14   *(Beat.)* **Anyway, I have to go. I have a date.**
15   *(She turns to leave, then stops and looks back over her*
16   *shoulder with a wry smile.)* **Yes ... even me.**

King Hedley II
by August Wilson

1   *Ruby, a mature African American woman who was a former*
2   *big-band singer, is the devoted and fiercely loyal wife of King*
3   *Hedley II, an alienated recluse of a harsh environment that*
4   *has thwarted his potential and left all his dreams deferred.*
5   *Here, Ruby recalls an incident that happened after she*
6   *stopped singing and explores her struggle to come to terms*
7   *with personal anguish and advancing age.*
8

9   RUBY: I stopped singing. I just stopped for no reason.
10   I did it to myself. Said, "I don't want to sing no more."
11   It had done lost something. The melody or something, I
12   couldn't tell. I just know it stopped having any meaning
13   for me. There was lots of things like that. Where the
14   meaning all got mixed up with something else.
15   After I quit singing my hair turned gray. My hair
16   turned gray and I didn't even know it. I was staying in a
17   room up on Wooster Street. I went upstairs to the
18   bathroom and seen I had gray hair. Seem like I didn't
19   have nothing to show for it. I said, "I'm gonna die and
20   ain't nobody gonna miss me." I don't know what it was.
21   I got dressed and said, "I'm going go find me a man. If
22   nothing else he might miss me in the morning when I'm
23   gone." We went to the Ellis Hotel. He had a moustache
24   and a big hat. It was that hat that made him look nice.
25   He was a rough man. He turned me over his knee and
26   spanked me. That was the first time anybody ever did
27   that. He asked me did I like it. I told him I didn't know,
28   he'd have to do it again. It had been a long time since
29   anybody had touched me. It kinda felt good. Just to

1   know I had been touched. We had a good time. Then it was
2   time to go. I asked him if he was gonna miss me. He said
3   he was, but I don't know if he was telling the truth. I went
4   back and looked in the mirror and my hair was still gray.
5   I told myself, "I'm still a woman. Gray hair and all."

Glass Trees
by Peggy Dunne

1　*Noelle, a gifted photographer, shelved a promising*
2　*professional career to care for her ailing alcoholic mother.*
3　*Now, five years later, her mother has slipped into a coma,*
4　*and Noelle is stretched to the breaking point. At her mother's*
5　*bedside, much to her own surprise, a courageous Noelle*
6　*experiences a poignant emotional breakthrough and reveals*
7　*the passion and uncommon honesty that often surface in*
8　*times of despair.*

9

10　**NOELLE:** Yesterday morning I woke up and it looked
11　like someone poured glass over the whole city. Every
12　tree, branch, and twig was covered by a layer of crystal
13　ice. Every knot, bend, hole, and bump. It's not that I've
14　never seen that before, but usually it melts by midday,
15　you know? But there was no sun yesterday, so last
16　night, everything — the streets, the buildings, telephone
17　poles, electric lines, everything — was still encased in
18　ice.
19　　I took a walk. Cars were abandoned by their drivers;
20　not a single person was out. When the wind blew, the
21　branches clinked and tapped like the sound of dainty
22　bones. I carefully ran my hand over the smooth limbs. I
23　hardly dared to breathe. It seemed at any moment they
24　would shatter and collapse in a heap. At that moment,
25　I realized ... I haven't taken a breath in five years, Mom.
26　I've been terrified that — everything's felt so fragile —
27　that I would crumble and break into a million pieces and
28　I'd ...
29　　So, I batted at a branch, heavy and thick with ice,

1   at first gingerly, but nothing happened. I swatted at it
2   harder, and the ice cracked and fell to the ground. Then I
3   ran to another tree, my feet slipping and sliding
4   underneath me, and took a swing at it. Ice crashed to the
5   ground. I took hold of the small trunk and shook the tree
6   hard, and ice chunks fell on my head and shoulders and
7   face and the tops of my feet. Then I ran to a huge
8   evergreen tree — as fast as I could on the slick ice — and
9   just as I reached it, my feet propelled out from underneath
10 me, and I dove into the tree head first. I hugged it to brace
11 my fall and the weight of my body crushed and cracked
12 the ice. It scratched and scraped my face, but the
13 branches underneath were soft, and I could smell the fresh
14 green needles — it was strange to feel pain and comfort at
15 the same time. Then I shook it and swung at it and dove
16 back into it. Ice was flying and falling everywhere, it pinged
17 against windows, crawled down inside the back of my
18 coat, chunks stuck to my hair.
19   Then, a porch light turned on and I froze. An old man
20 stepped out of the front door, in his robe and slippers.
21 "Who's there?" he asked. I didn't answer. I got an image
22 of myself buried in this icy tree with just my feet
23 protruding out of the bottom, and I suddenly had an urge
24 to bust out laughing. My shoulders started shaking, like
25 when you're in church and you laugh even harder for fear
26 of being found out and yelled at by the priest. Eileen and I
27 did that all the time, remember? I pressed my face into the
28 branches to stifle my laughter. You know that feeling? Like
29 you don't know if you're laughing or crying and feel that
30 you've, for an instant, lost your mind? The man went back
31 inside and turned the porch light off. I waited. I could see
32 him looking out of his window — he looked ghostly, his
33 skin a transparent blue — trying to see what was in his
34 tree. I slowly slid down the tree and crawled away and ran
35 back home. *(Pause.)*

Fabulation
by Lynn Nottage

1 *Undine, a mature, African American businesswoman, is talking*
2 *to her sympathetic friend Allison as a crew of burly men hastily*
3 *repossess her office furniture. She had been a successful head*
4 *of a prosperous public relations firm, until her double-dealing*
5 *husband ran away with all her money. Now, Undine is feeling*
6 *the pangs of guilt and retribution for having been a little too*
7 *pleased with her success in life.*
8
9 **UNDINE:** No one seems troubled by the actual charges
10 against me. No, the crime isn't being a criminal, it's being
11 broke. It's apparently against the law to be a poor black
12 woman in New York City.
13   *(Whispered)* They auctioned off my furniture. It was like
14 a feeding frenzy, people I knew bidding on my possessions
15 waving little flags and purchasing bits and pieces of my life
16 for a bargain.
17   At some point I thought they were actually going to
18 put me up on the block and sell me to the highest bidder.
19 And in a flash I thought, "Thank God I got my teeth done
20 last year." "Look at them teeth, she got a fine set of teeth
21 y'all." How naive, foolish of me to assume that I was
22 worthy of some comfort and good fortune, a better chance.
23 They give you a taste, "How ya like it?" then promptly take
24 it away. "Oh, I'm sorry, we've reached our quota of
25 Negroes in the privileged class, unfortunately we're
26 bumping you down to working class." Working. I'm not
27 even working. I think I'm officially part of the underclass.
28 Penniless. I've returned to my original Negro state, karmic
29 retribution for feeling a bit too pleased with my life.

In a Tired City
by Gus Edwards

1   *In a heartfelt, wrenching exploration of human misery and*
2   *suffering set against the searing panorama of a tired city, a*
3   *nameless African American woman searches relentlessly for*
4   *meaning in her life. It is a pathetic tale of becoming*
5   *hopelessly ensnarled in a cold, impersonal world of towering*
6   *buildings and miles of crumbling streets, with a disturbing*
7   *view of the human spirit's inability to survive in such an*
8   *asphalt and concrete world.*
9

10   **WOMAN:** So — you go out and walk through the
11   streets of the tired city. Looking for hope. But hope is
12   something that's hard to find. So you look for dreams,
13   but dreams ain't nowhere to be found either.
14   Then go back to your room, take off your dress, and
15   think about lying down for a while. 'Cause if you lie down
16   then you might fall asleep. And sleep is the only place
17   where hope and dreams have any kind of chance in this
18   tired city.
19   Then you change your mind and decide to look out
20   the window one more time at this collection of buildings
21   and streets that pretends it cares. But that's all it is, a
22   game of pretend. 'Cause it don't really give a damn. Not
23   about anything. Or anyone. It never did, and never
24   will ... Not about me, not about you, not about the nine-
25   to-fivers who go to work every day. Or the holy ones who
26   pray and watch TV every night. They is all lost souls
27   floating in this fish tank we call life. Swimming around
28   in circles, never getting anywhere except to where we
29   been before. Endlessly swimming but not getting any

1   place. Any place at all.
2   Folks talk about a town without pity, but this is a city
3   without a heart. All it has is the mouth to take you in,
4   chew you up, taste you a little bit, and then spit you out.
5   People live in this city. But more of them die. Some by
6   liquor, others by dope, hope, or bad dreams. And then all
7   the rest by cancer or some other rotting disease. God help
8   me, I live here but I want out so bad I could taste it. I could
9   just taste it.

Vamp
by Ry Herman

1   *Shortly after she is "out-ed" as a vampire, Angela decides to*
2   *give a public lecture designed to puncture the false beliefs*
3   *and faulty myths commonly held about vampires. Her lecture*
4   *is thoroughly polished and vividly drawn with lethal and*
5   *macabre humor, but turns deadly serious when she begins to*
6   *describe a recent bloodsucking relationship of her own.*
7
8   ANGELA: Um, hi. I was, uh, thinking it might be a good
9   idea right now to have a little talk about vampires.
10   Vampires seem to be pretty much everywhere these
11 days, right? I mean, they're in books, they're in films,
12 they're on TV — and so most people probably think they
13 have a pretty good handle on what vampires are all
14 about. But actually, there's a lot of misinformation out
15 there, and a lot of big gaps in what "everybody knows."
16 Let's take television, OK? I mean, nearly every vampire
17 you see on TV is the European Dracula type. Think
18 about it, when was the last time you saw an Asian
19 hopping vampire or an African *mumiani** on a show? It's
20 like they don't even exist.
21   And the U.S. Census still doesn't even have a
22 "vampire" category, so nobody even really knows
23 exactly how many there are. And it's not easy to
24 estimate, because it's almost impossible to tell the
25 difference between a town with vampires and a town
26 where people just happen to bite each other a lot. What
27 I'm trying to say is, most people really know a lot less

---

*In Asian vampire myths, rigor mortis prevents vampires from bending their knees, so they move by hopping. As a result, vampires weirdly bouncing around is a common staple of many Asian horror films. The *mumiani* (moo me a ne) is an African version of the vampire legend. The word originally referred to a kind of medicinal gum, but a belief that the substance was made from blood eventually led to the word becoming associated with blood-drinking monsters.

1   about vampires than they think they do.
2   So, I'd like to start by dispelling a few common
3   vampire myths. Myth number one: Everyone a vampire
4   bites becomes a vampire. This is a totally ridiculous idea.
5   I mean, just do the math. Say you start with just one
6   vampire. Even if vampires only bite someone once a
7   month, that means everyone in the world would be a
8   vampire in under three years. Actually, turning people into
9   vampires is, trust me, a long and complicated procedure.
10   Which is why, instead of being surrounded by vampires
11   right now, you're surrounded by werewolves.
12   Myth number two: Vampires kill their victims. This one
13   probably does more damage to the reputation of vampires
14   than anything else. I mean, if you're prejudiced, this is
15   probably why, right? But it's just crazy. Where are the
16   reports of morgues filled with bloodless corpses with neck
17   hickeys? Actually, vampires don't have to kill anyone at
18   all, necessarily. You see, there's only so much a vampire
19   can drink at a time, and it's just not enough to do real
20   damage. They're actually sort of like vegetarians, except
21   they don't even murder vegetables.
22   Myth number three: All vampires suck blood. In fact,
23   vampires feed in all kinds of different ways. Some of them,
24   for example, can use practically any bodily fluid at all. But,
25   let's not go there. There are other vampires that are
26   actually allergic to blood, and have to make do with a
27   variety of soy-based blood substitutes. And some don't
28   feed on anything even resembling blood. That kind usually
29   starts out by telling you that they love you. And when they
30   do, things can be really great, at first, anyway.
31   But after a while, things start to go wrong. They get
32   kind of cold, or they get angry for no reason. But you
33   figure, hey, every relationship has problems, right? So you
34   try to talk it out, make everything happy again. But things
35   get worse. You don't know why. Everything's going wrong,

1   and somehow it's your fault. You're not doing it right.
2   You're not loving enough. If you loved them enough,
3   everything would be fine, but it's not, so you need to love
4   them more and more, but it never seems to be enough,
5   and you just think, "What's wrong with me?" If I'd just
6   been loving enough, everything would have been all right,
7   but I couldn't, I didn't have it in me, because I'm a bad,
8   mean person and I can't really love anybody. I can't ...
9   I can't ...

Kiss Me Again
by Bruce Kellner

1   *In this non-dramatic memoir text, Fritzi Scheff, legendary*
2   *opera and later cabaret singer at the Café Grinzing, wears a*
3   *faded silk dressing gown as she sits posed for an interview*
4   *with a local reporter. In response to questions, she is at once*
5   *the actress and the diva — petulant, funny, imperious, and*
6   *sometimes almost unbearable. Fritzi is also slightly hearing*
7   *impaired, and must occasionally ask "what" or "hmmm"*
8   *before answering a question.*
9
10 **FRITZI: Now, we have tea, my dear! I am so sorry not**
11 **to have more time for you this afternoon for — what is**
12 **your newspaper? No, no, magazine, you said. I hope it**
13 **wants my picture.** *(A self-deprecating laugh and pose)* **My**
14 **pictures are better than my words for interview. I never**
15 **know what to answer to so many questions, and my**
16 **words fly about like arias and perhaps they are not**
17 **translating into your oh, so cold-hearted typing on the**
18 **pages. But I try to answer your questions and I try to**
19 **behave. Yes?**
20 *(She pours out two cups of tea through some of this*
21 *chatter and, ostensibly anyway, she gives one to her guest*
22 *by placing it on the corner of the desk near him.)*
23 **What?** *(Her attention drawn to one of the posters)* **Oh,**
24 **that one is** *Babette.* **Wasn't I beautiful? Mr. Herbert made**
25 **it for me especially. What? Who?** *Victor* **Herbert!** *Lieber*
26 *Gott!* **You are so young! You don't know Victor Herbert?**
27 **He was a great composer, darling! He made all of my**
28 **roles for me especially — well, not all of my roles but**
29 **some of my roles, my great roles, and — that one?**

1	*(Another poster)* **Oh, you know that one, that one is my —**
2	**my — you know, my** *Kiss Me Again,* **my** *Mademoiselle*
3	*Modiste***!** *(She begins to sing it, then laughs at herself; her*
4	*soprano voice is remarkably clear for a woman her age, a little*
5	*frayed perhaps but still quite lovely.)*
6	**Sweet summer breeze,**
7	**Whispering trees,**
8	**Stars shining brightly above ...**
9	**Twenty-six encores on opening night! Christmas night,**
10	**19 —** *lieber Gott!* **1906! Oh, I forgot the biscuits!** *(She leaps*
11	*and runs toward the kitchen, but the interviewer's question*
12	*stops her and she forgets about the biscuits.)*
13	**What? Yes, that's the one I was singing last night at**
14	**the café when the — incident occurred. It has not before**
15	**happened to me, and the old gentleman was very gallant**
16	**to say that about me. But to interrupt Fritzi Scheff! In the**
17	**middle of** *Kiss Me Again* **to say that I was a great star and**
18	**should not be singing in such a common place, that I**
19	**should be enshrined there — yes, I remember everything**
20	**he said — even in the middle of** *Kiss Me Again!* **It is —**
21	**compliment even if it is coming at the wrong time. I**
22	**mean — it is flattering to me, no? To know that I am not**
23	**forgotten. That some of the people coming to dinner know**
24	**who I was — no, no, know who I** *am.* **I am still "the little**
25	**devil." Paderewski called me that once — you know**
26	**Paderewski! — and then everybody called me that:**
27	**"naughty little devil" and "good little devil," "the little devil**
28	**of Grand Opera," but I was not temperamental!**
29	**Emotional, yes, temperamental, no!**
30	**But temperament! Temperament makes an artist! It**
31	**is — attitude; it is — concentration; it is —** *je ne sais quoi;*
32	**it is — "Fritzi!" And those other stories! That I paid an**
33	**electrician one hundred twenty dollars a week — big**
34	**money then! — just to keep my name in lights on my**
35	**dressing room door! Foolishness! He did it for free! And**

1   they made a big thing of the private railroad car I had on
2   trains. Why not? Everybody had private cars. But the story
3   that I suspended traffic on a Texas railroad because the
4   motion of the train made my bathwater spill over the sides
5   is ridiculous. I just asked sweetly for them to slow down
6   until I was completed in my toilette, and they were so
7   happy to do that for me. Also, I was making four thousand
8   dollars a week from Victor Herbert! Four thousand dollars
9   in 1906 was a lot of money!
10   Now maybe I make four dollars in tips on a good night
11   at the Café Grinzing, and — *(A sudden haunt)* after Café
12   Grinzing *(A quick recovery)* — oh, they don't fire me, they
13   like me — but who knows? Listen to me, darling, life upon
14   the wicked stage is very precarious ...

Runaway Home
by Darren J. Butler

1 *Pyper, a shy and withdrawn young girl teetering on the brink*
2 *of self-destruction, suffers insults and emotional abuse daily*
3 *at the hands of Natalie, an intolerable snob and bully. After*
4 *years of being victimized, Pyper finds the courage she had*
5 *been lacking for most of her life and confronts Natalie. Fear*
6 *and hysteria drive her to an inexplicable act of defiance ...*
7 *Pyper pulls a gun on Natalie.*
8
9 **PYPER: So, what are you looking at? I know what**
10 **you're thinking. You want to know why? Right? Everyone**
11 **wants to know that ... why? Well, I'll tell you why. I just**
12 **couldn't take it anymore. Sounds like a cop-out, right?**
13 **But you know what I mean. You've been there. Sure you**
14 **have. You know like when someone keeps doing**
15 **something to you over and over and over and you get to**
16 **the point that you just can't take it any longer and then**
17 **you ... you just snap. You have to stand up for yourself**
18 **and take care of business. See. You know what I'm**
19 **talking about. Or, maybe you don't. Maybe you're one of**
20 **those who just lets it slide. Is that how you are? Uh,**
21 **huh. Well, not me.**
22 **'Course everyone was shocked. You see, before this**
23 **happened I kind of had this reputation of being a quiet,**
24 **shy little thing that just kind of existed at that school.**
25 **No one took notice of me. Before this happened I would**
26 **have bet you a hundred bucks that I could have walked**
27 **through the hallway at that school wearing only my**
28 **smile, and no one would have noticed me.**
29 **Now, they can't stop talking about me. I'm the topic**

1   of conversation at the water fountain, the hallway, the
2   locker room. Now who would have ever thought that? Me,
3   the topic of conversation in the boy's locker room, now
4   that's something. Things sure do change quickly. They
5   changed pretty quick for Natalie Coleman, that's for sure.
6   You should have seen the look on her face. That snobby,
7   holier-than-thou smirk on her face changed into total
8   terror inside of a second. 'Course, when you're staring
9   down the barrel of a pistol, that'll happen to ya.
10   Now you're wondering again. You want to know how I
11   felt holding that gun up to her like that. Well, I'll tell ya. I
12   felt in control. I felt power ... So why didn't I do it? Why
13   didn't I just blow her brains out? I ain't got an answer for
14   that. For ten years she had been teasing me, talking about
15   me, putting me down, and I tell ya, I wanted to hurt her. I
16   wanted to hurt her bad. But I just couldn't pull the trigger.
17   I just stood there. I never took my eyes off her and she
18   never took her eyes off me. We'd been standing there for
19   probably fifteen minutes when the policeman took the gun
20   out of my hands. Even then ... I just kept staring at her.

She Says
by Bara Swain

1   *Ms. Pink, a colorful and mature "Southern lady" with a folksy*
2   *homespun manner, speaks lovingly of her Grandma Bitty*
3   *from Arkansas and her devotion to Grandpa Willie. It is a*
4   *deeply moving yarn of friendship and dying that serves as a*
5   *sterling tribute to Grandma Bitty, who put her own life on*
6   *hold to care for Grandpa Willie so he could die with a*
7   *measure of dignity.*
8
9   **MS. PINK: My Grandma Bitty from Arkansas? She**
10 **buried two dogs, a copy of** Lassie Come Home, **and**
11 **Grandpa Willie right outside her kitchen window, smack**
12 **in the middle of her favorite azalea bushes. Some folk**
13 **say she had the purtiest backyard west of the**
14 **Mississippi! Two ... three acres of wildflowers and a**
15 **weeping willow that only cried at births and weddings,**
16 **Grandpa Willie used to say. Though he never said much.**
17 **And after his stroke? He never spoke again.**
18 **(Silence.) For the next two years Grandma Bitty**
19 **stayed by his side, tending to him like her prized**
20 **begonias, fussin' over him like a first-born. For two**
21 **years she never set foot outside her own front door. But**
22 **every evening she'd slip out back and visit that old**
23 **willow ... wrap her arms around its trunk ... and whisper**
24 **knock-knock jokes. That willow never stopped weeping**
25 **'til the morning he died.**
26 **(Pause. Then she laughs.) I rolled nineteen dollars**
27 **worth of pennies the day Grandpa Willie got his wings.**
28 **Poor Mama — she locked herself in her bedroom with a**
29 **box of Fig Newtons and the family album. And Grandma**

1   Bitty? She walked nine miles to town, joined Jack
2   LaLanne and the Democratic Club, and bought her first
3   pair of panty hose.
4   *(She wavers.)* Grandma Bitty would've moved heaven
5   and earth for that man. Ohhhh, she loved him so!

Better Places to Go
by David-Matthew Barnes

1   *Neurotic and high-strung, Candace is running late for her*
2   *own wedding and on the verge of a total collapse. Waiting*
3   *out a threatening storm in a run-down ramshackle diner in*
4   *Grand Island, Nebraska, Candace is filled with bitter rage and*
5   *can barely take a breath as she unleashes a barrage of self-*
6   *wounding insults about herself and her horrible day on an*
7   *unsuspecting bus boy.*
8
9   CANDACE: Do you know what kind of a day I've had? I
10 woke up late. My cat puked all over my shoes. My
11 roommate decided to bring a criminal home with her
12 last night and the guy stole her virginity *(Pauses)* and *my*
13 laptop. The landlord forgot to inform me that they were
14 shutting off the water in my building to do some *repair*
15 *work.* So I had to boil bottles of Aquafina and wash my
16 hair in the sink. A necklace my grandmother gave me
17 fell down the drain and is probably lying at the bottom
18 of Lake Michigan right now. I got locked out of my
19 apartment, so I took the "L" train to Maxine's house —
20 *in my wedding dress* and my cat-puke satin pumps. I
21 didn't get a manicure, so my hands look like I've been
22 clawing my way out of Africa. My hair feels like Crisco
23 because my hairdresser decided to try a *new* product on
24 me, and I swear to you, it smells like furniture polish. We
25 missed the plane from Chicago, and once we finally got
26 on a plane, they rerouted us to Topeka because of some
27 storm, but I don't see any rain, *do you*? My own mother
28 is refusing to talk to me because I wouldn't allow my
29 slutty sister to be in my wedding. My father has been

1   missing for three days, and we suspect he's joined a
2   religious cult in Arkansas. My fiancé thinks I'm a fat cow,
3   an alcoholic, a drug addict, and a chain smoker. And right
4   now, all I want to do is be *unconscious!*

Radio Ball
by Lauren Kettler

1   *Tommy, a gifted Japanese American high school athlete,*
2   *dreamed of playing professional baseball. Her best friend and*
3   *practice partner, Robin — Pee Wee, as she called him — is now*
4   *a college baseball pitcher on the cusp of professional success.*
5   *Here, Pee Wee conjures up the voice and vision of Tommy from*
6   *his adolescent past. Even though he can no longer see his*
7   *friend and muse, Pee Wee hears her voice and, finally, accepts*
8   *the spirit and inspiration behind it.*
9
10 **TOMMY:** *(Tommy stands in her practice clothes, the wind*
11 *apparently knocked out of her, a baseball bat in her hand.)* **You**
12 **don't want to hang around here, Pee Wee, you're supposed**
13 **to be at practice. And whatever you do, you don't want to**
14 **be late for practice. It's really bad form, and the people don't**
15 **like it. But thanks for coming by and checking on me, Pee**
16 **Wee. I told you, you don't have to feel bad that you made it**
17 **and I didn't. Like the poet Basho said, "Year after year / on**
18 **the monkey's face / a monkey's face." That's just the way**
19 **it is. Some things never change, you know? Like ancient**
20 **sports traditions and dim-witted science teachers. But I saw**
21 **what you did for me, that crazy pitch you came up with right**
22 **after they made me leave the field. Too bad they weren't**
23 **clocking it, it blew by the batter so fast I thought it was**
24 **going to knock him over. You know what they used to call**
25 **that? A radio ball. You know why? It's so fast you can hear**
26 **it but you can't see it. My grandma, my Sobo, would call**
27 **that a tsunami ball. It's like a tidal wave, they don't even**
28 **know what hit them. Thanks, Pee Wee, for throwing that**
29 **crazy tsunami ball in my honor.**

1 *(She bows.)* **Even though you didn't really mean to, did**
2 **you? You just got mad because they kicked me out, that's**
3 **why you threw it. You were on fire. I like that side of you, Pee**
4 **Wee. I like it when you let yourself go. I guess we really**
5 **showed them, huh? At least they let me play long enough to**
6 **show them a few things. Did you see their faces when I**
7 **planted two in a row over the bleachers? It didn't matter**
8 **though. They weren't going to let me join if I out-hit and out-**
9 **fielded every boy on the team. But some of the players were**
10 **nice to me afterward. You know the guy on third, Tyco? He**
11 **asked for my phone number. How's that for a booby prize?**
12 **You can't be on the Varsity team, but you can date the**
13 **Varsity third baseman.**
14 *(Takes out a cigarette to hold.)* **You know what I was**
15 **thinking about before you came? You know how in baseball**
16 **we're always trying to do the same exact thing over and over**
17 **again? Trying to relive that one moment when we connected**
18 **with the ball just right? Off the field, you never get two**
19 **moments that are exactly the same, ever. We'll probably**
20 **never have this moment again. You know what I mean? This**
21 **could be our moment, Pee Wee. This could be it. You could**
22 **kiss me right now and find out. You could do that. If you**
23 **want. Right now. You could kiss me, Robin.**
24 *(She closes her eyes expectantly. When she opens them,*
25 *moments later, she takes out some matches and lights her*
26 *cigarette, coughing it up in the process.)* **You know what I'm**
27 **really not good at is waiting, like when you're standing at the**
28 **plate and you're waiting for your pitch. Sadaharu Oh, the**
29 **greatest Japanese slugger of all time, wrote how waiting is**
30 **the most active state of all. But I definitely don't excel in that**
31 **area. So if you're not going to kiss me, Pee Wee, the least**
32 **you can do is pitch to me. Come on, give me your best shot.**
33 **Let's see that world-famous tsunami ball of yours. Let's see**
34 **it. Come on. Throw it!** *(Too loud)* **Now!**

Vain Attempt
by LaShea Delaney

1   *Joy, a pale young girl with a hollow look of emptiness in her*
2   *blank eyes, has always been judged more on her surface*
3   *beauty than on her inner virtues. Now, in the aftermath of a*
4   *vicious knife attack that has disfigured her, Joy must*
5   *struggle to survive not only the shattering trauma of living life*
6   *without the "perfect" face, but also the brutal reality that only*
7   *she can save herself.*
8

9   **JOY:** *(Lights up on a hospital room. The whole area is very*
10   *sterile and chrome. It looks a lot like an operating room with*
11   *very white walls and very sharp lines. Joy lies in the middle*
12   *of a gurney. She lays still at first and then begins to writhe*
13   *around as if she were having a bad dream. She sits up and*
14   *begins to clutch at her bandaged face, slowly removing the*
15   *gauze.)* **When I was sixteen I was hit by a car. I was**
16   **crossing the street on the way to school and this man**
17   **just sped through a red light and hit me. I can**
18   **remember that sensation of flying through the air, and**
19   **then that's it, that's all I can remember. When I woke up**
20   **my mother was standing over me with a smile on her**
21   **face and she said to me, "Your leg is broken and so are**
22   **two of your ribs, but look on the bright side, your face**
23   **is still beautiful." When I got out of the hospital my**
24   **mother took me home and there were family and friends**
25   **waiting for me with a get-well-soon party, and a part of**
26   **me knew that if my face had been broken instead of my**
27   **ribs no one would have been there.**
28   *(Pause.)* **Since the incident and leaving the hospital I**
29   **have these dreams. I wake up in the middle of the night**

1 and walk to the bathroom, everything is dark, and when I
2 turn on the bathroom light everything is normal. My face
3 is still beautiful, but there is a dirt smudge on my cheek,
4 and I start to scrub it harder and harder and then I look in
5 the mirror again and my face is bleeding. My forehead, my
6 nose, my cheeks, and then my face starts to slowly melt,
7 and I am trying to hold it all together but I can't, and I
8 begin to scream. I wake up in a cold sweat and examine
9 my face and I can feel the jagged rise and fall of my
10 cheeks. I can remember what the knife felt like when it
11 slashed through my lovely skin. I can remember the people
12 around me watching but not moving. I can feel his hand on
13 my shoulder knowing now that I should have run.
14   *(Pause.)* When I'm in the grocery store and I can feel
15 people watching me and wondering what happened, or
16 when I'm at a makeup counter and no one lifts a hand to
17 help me, I sometimes think that I would have both my legs
18 and all of my ribs broken just to have my face again. When
19 I came home from the hospital there was no one there to
20 greet me. My mother walked me into my tiny bedroom,
21 helped me into bed, and tried her best not to look at me.
22 I think that's the worst part — no one knows where to look
23 when they talk to me; wandering eyes trying not to stare.
24 Or maybe the worst part is the envy has been replaced by
25 pity when I look into their eyes.
26   *(Pause.)* My mother came over yesterday to make me
27 some soup and to ask why I have become a hermit, and
28 the last thing she said before she left was, "Your hands are
29 still beautiful."

Sea of Tranquility
by Howard Korder

1 *Astarte, a snappy young girl estranged from her family, is a*
2 *vagabond searching for a better life. Her journey so far has*
3 *been feast or famine, brief periods of unrestrained freedom or*
4 *extended periods of loneliness. Wandering through the dark,*
5 *grubby underworld of addicts and derelicts, Astarte's perilous*
6 *misadventures are sometimes chilly and frightening. Here she*
7 *recalls an incident with Donald, a shadowy figure she met*
8 *while sitting in the emergency room of a Los Angeles hospital*
9 *following a vicious attack.*
10
11 ASTARTE: I was sitting in the emergency room,
12 because, um, I'd been sleeping in Griffith Park, because
13 I'd been living in the truck, because I'd stopped paying
14 the rent, so I'd moved into the truck, because I wouldn't
15 go home. But the truck got towed, so I was sleeping in
16 the park, that made sense, even though it was obviously
17 completely wrong, and I'd been, ha, stabbed actually by
18 two guys trying to rape me to be honest, one of them
19 kind of sliced my calf open as a parting gesture, so,
20 emergency room, shaking, this man says to me,
21 tetracycline. "Are you a doctor?" because he doesn't
22 look like one, maybe thirty, sort of FBI suit, and he
23 says, "What the health-care hegemony conspires to
24 keep secret is that a wide variety of illnesses can be
25 addressed by the well-informed layman. Every person
26 has the power to make himself better." And something
27 in his voice, very sure but not asking me to agree, I saw
28 he wanted me to come with him, and everything would
29 be all right. "Donald."

1   He had, really an awful lot of drugs in a refrigerator in
2   his garage, the Physician's Desk Reference, he said, "I'm
3   going to wash you and irrigate you and sew you up. I'm
4   sensing other issues too, serotonin levels, emotions are
5   chemical, you can change who you are." He put me to bed,
6   in a room with a poster of a covered bridge and this quality
7   of total blankness, like no one had ever felt anything in it,
8   no sadness or happiness or confusion, it just canceled out
9   everything inside. I woke up, the house was empty, just
10 stacks of binders with titles like "Arc Straightwire,"
11 "False Purpose Rundown." Card table with some kind of
12 quiz, little Post-It on top: "Please fill this out." "Do you
13 speak slowly," "Would you rather give orders than take
14 them," on and on two hundred questions. I looked up,
15 there was Donald. "What do you make of it?" "Well, you're
16 supposed to feel something's wrong with you, no matter
17 how you answer."
18   And he, like almost a smile. So for every person I can
19 get to fill one out, he'll give me four dollars, could I
20 manage that? What happens then? "I offer them the
21 chance to transform their lives." Really? How? Why is
22 there sorrow in this world, he asks me. And I think about
23 the room, the nothing room, where you don't want or hope
24 or expect, and suddenly I'm in pieces, like I've never cried
25 in my life except when I was born, maybe, and he says,
26 "don't worry, it's only chemical, we'll start you on Zoloft
27 and lithium, be patient, at least six weeks, meanwhile can
28 you do what I ask? It will be good for you and good for me."
29 Every morning he took me to a different park of L.A., and
30 I'd pick the likeliest ones, the fat, the pockmarked, the
31 guy with the zipper half-open, be sweet and charming and
32 make four dollars. I liked it. How clear. How easy. You
33 could tell people almost anything you wanted about
34 themselves. And they'd believe you. Because they don't
35 know any better. Do they. *(Pause.)*

Watbanaland
by Doug Wright

1   *Flo Stillman, a nursery school teacher desperate to have*
2   *children of her own, is saddled with a chilly, distant*
3   *husband whose secret affair with his secretary resulted in the*
4   *birth of a brain-damaged child. Flo, blissfully unaware of her*
5   *husband's affair, begins to compulsively adopt Third World*
6   *children through late-night "infomercials" on television and*
7   *becomes increasingly obsessed with her imagined*
8   *responsibility to nurture the world's underprivileged. Her life*
9   *takes a surreal turn, however, when she endures a phantom*
10   *pregnancy after a miraculous visit from Third World*
11   *emissaries.*
12
13   **FLO:** *(Flo sits on her stool, holding a picture book. She*
14   *wears a few African bracelets and an elephant-hair necklace.*
15   *She is quite obviously pregnant.)* **"So Mr. Dingle pulled up**
16   **his bootstraps and said to the cabbage, 'My, oh my but**
17   **you're leafy and green!' The cabbage rolled its eyes and**
18   **shook its head and moaned its cabbage moan ..."**
19   *(In the distance, the remote roar of a giant cat. The light*
20   *turns a blazing white. Flo is distracted, then continues*
21   *reading.)* **"Mr. Dingle had never been in the mysterious**
22   **garden before, and he had never heard a cabbage**
23   **wail ..."**
24   *(The rattle of drums. Flo stops cold.)* **Shhhh. Class.**
25   **Listen.**
26   *(Flo closes the book.)* **Do you remember the stick**
27   **baby? That's right. Baku. And where is Baku from? It's**
28   **a long word. Ruthie, yes. Watbanaland. Ruthie gets a**
29   **gold star. As we sit in air-conditioned comfort, reading**

1   this colorful book, diverting ourselves from the world
2   outside, what do you suppose Baku is doing? Tending the
3   goats? Maybe, if there are goats to tend. Grinding millet?
4   Perhaps, if the crops did not burn. Suppose we could
5   invite Baku to be here, with us, in the nursery. Suppose
6   we could share snack time with Baku. We'd give him a
7   napkin, and a big, tall glass of orange juice. Yes. Fresh-
8   squeezed. And what would Baku do? He'd drink that juice
9   right down, to ward off scurvy, to fatten his brittle
10 bones — his bones like thermometers, his mouth like a
11 gaping wound. He'd suck it down fast, because back
12 home, in Watbanaland, the land is parched and unable to
13 bring forth fruit. When we look into his eyes, his round,
14 saucer eyes, what do we see? A vast, inner cavern of want.
15 Want so large it terrifies. A hunger so rapacious that if we
16 don't hold fast to the furniture, we, too, shall be sucked
17 under and devoured.
18   *(Flo stretches out her hand.)* Ruthie, Mrs. Stillman is
19 shaking. Hold Mrs. Stillman's hand.
20   *(A faraway cry. Flo closes her eyes.)* Did you hear that?
21 On the wind, across the sand, a cry. Another baby being
22 born.
23   *(Flo cups her rounded belly. Two sharp intakes of breath.*
24 *She sits, stone-still. The sound dies away. The lights are*
25 *restored, Flo sighs deeply, then opens her eyes.)* Where were
26 we?
27   *(She opens the book and resumes reading.)* "'Good
28 gracious!' cried Mr. Dingle to the cabbage. 'I never heard
29 such a noise!' With that, the cabbage only groaned more
30 loudly, so the carrots quivered and the rutabaga shook
31 with fear..." *(Blackout.)*

Chapter 6

Shattered Mirrors:
Fire and Ice

"Weep not for the silent dead. Their pain
is past … ours is just beginning."
— Helen D'Arcy Cranston, *Song of Genius*

These fire-and-ice characters from full-length playscripts are engulfed by the flames of anguish, or stand rigid and frozen in the past, as they try to put the pieces of their lives back together again. They carry with them the precious ashes of failed dreams, emotional lacerations, and unspeakable nightmares. Although there are occasional outbursts of fleeting joy, for the most part these road-weary characters are on their final journey home. They are accompanied by fellow traveling companions: guilt, regret, and silence. They burn with a passion to understand the meaning of their lives and then freeze with self-effacing humor to mask an antic behavior.

Constantly gasping for a breath of fresh air, they suffocate on their painful memories … and then lie down to sleep. But do not weep for these silent dead. The understanding that they have gained about themselves is profound, and in these compelling stories we see their courage to face adversity and wrestle with their own fate. They focus our attention on human vulnerability, and take us to those secret places within our own minds which most of us have chosen not to visit.

As you consider these stories, pay careful attention to surface details, minor flaws, and simple actions. These will provide the backdrop against which the "inner truths" of the characters' lives surface. The playwrights here provide a sometimes raw and somber slice of life, so it is important to look more closely at the shifting tides of frustration and passion that motivate the characters to perform rash or even irrational deeds. Remember, as well, that these characters define their own values, act in accordance with their own principles, and wish to be understood on their own terms.

In playing the character roles of fire and ice, your performance will need to be restrained. Focus on attitude, mood, and self-image to highlight character individuality. Be sensitive to their despair or disappointment, but do not glorify or romanticize their suffering with a performance of undisciplined emotion. The characters here are too carefully and credibly drawn for a one-dimensional, stereotypical performance.

Some attention should also be paid to each character's spontaneous reactions in the given circumstances in the text to avoid repetitive physical or vocal responses that could become predictable in performance. Limited stage movement may be more effective in these portraits to subtly suggest intense moments of "distance" or "separation" in character action or attitude. Finally, you should approach these challenging roles with a passion to voice each character's story free of false sentiments, and with no emotional or intellectual indecision.

no known country
by Steven Schutzman

1 *Birdwoman, an exploited and abused sexual captive in a war*
2 *of ethnic cleansing, stands center stage over the bodies of her*
3 *two captors who have just shot each other dead and speaks*
4 *softly in a matter-of-fact tone directly to the audience. She*
5 *had willed herself to become a bird in order to escape the*
6 *reality of abuse she suffered, and now offers a dark and*
7 *troubled account of her mental and spiritual struggles.*
8
9 BIRDWOMAN: I never saw my original captors. I was
10 taken from my bed in the dark with a burlap bag shoved
11 onto my head. I didn't see the light of day for weeks. I
12 was raped repeatedly and lost consciousness
13 repeatedly. We traveled. I remember the winding of the
14 engine and the terrible bumping of unpaved roads in the
15 back of the truck where my body was being jostled
16 against other female bodies living and dead. I began to
17 dread those moments of tender weeping against another
18 living female body. Understanding that tenderness hurt
19 more than pain, I didn't try to find out whether anyone
20 was from my village. Eventually I forgot my name.
21 Whenever the truck stopped, I was assaulted
22 repeatedly. I believe we were being trucked around to
23 serve various camps. I tried to will myself to die but
24 couldn't. It's amazing what one's body will endure even
25 after you yourself have given up. As time went on I
26 became more and more skilled at flying away, at making
27 things distant as if they were happening in a far-off
28 world, the world where my body was and I was not
29 anymore. Finally I wound up in this small camp, and

1   things got better in some ways and worse in some ways.
2   Better that I was abused fewer times. Worse that there
3   was no more traveling and so I never knew when it would
4   happen and couldn't prepare myself to fly away. Better
5   that the soldiers removed the bag from my head, not
6   caring if I saw them because this meant they intended to
7   kill me soon. Worse that they forced me, my mouth,
8   choking on the sour taste of men living on roots and the
9   meat of stray dogs. Better that I eventually learned to
10   control my presence in their world with more precision.
11   Worse that there was another woman there for a while who
12   would hold me between violations and make me feel a
13   longing for life again. Here is a picture of the bodies of my
14   last captors who killed each other because of the sickness
15   they tried to transfer from their souls into mine.
16   *(BIRDWOMAN bites furiously at her skin like a bird*
17   *anxiously and compulsively picking at its feathers.)*

Training My Hands for War
by Matt Di Cintio

1   *Sunny, a young, idealistic, and warm-hearted prostitute is*
2   *forced to look more closely at her unremarkable life when she*
3   *catches a glimpse of herself reflected in a lover's mirrored*
4   *expression of bemusement. Sunny had dreams of being a*
5   *dancer, constantly in flight, fluid motion, and always on the*
6   *run. Now, she sees that the real tragedy is not how much her*
7   *world has changed, but how much it has remained the*
8   *same ... still on the run.*
9
10   SUNNY: What are you looking at? Don't look at me with
11   that face. I've seen that expression before. I've seen it a
12   million times before. Don't think I don't know what it
13   means. I know exactly what it means. All my life I've
14   been trying to get that look on my face, and I just can't
15   imagine it. Maybe it means I have too much heart.
16   Maybe it means I don't have any. My first lover, my only
17   real lover, the one with dark eyes, painted that look on
18   his face when he left me. It was that exact look, only his
19   eyebrows were raised a little more than that. As if it
20   were a surprise to him that he was saying goodbye. It
21   was a surprise to me. It's still a surprise to me. It's that
22   exact look my father wore when I told him what I needed
23   to be: on my own, free, unbound, all those things, yes.
24   But I needed to dance. I have to spend the rest of my
25   life moving. It was the motion, it was in the motion that
26   I was me. I have a vision in my mind of myself, and
27   whenever I picture myself I'm running. I'm running
28   home, I'm running away from home, I'm running to the
29   edge of the stage for my bow and my applause. And the

1   look I have on my face is nothing anybody has ever seen
2   anywhere before. Ever. It's the look of someone who's
3   gotten to where they're going. Do you know that look? I sat
4   across from my father with my feet in perfect fourth
5   position — under the table my feet were on the floor but
6   in my mind they were in the air in an arch I could have
7   taught classes about. The only arch at that table was the
8   one his eyebrows formed in confusion. He was, as the word
9   goes to describe it perfectly, *bemused*. The poor man who
10   wore looks easier than he wears cheap shoes. The poor
11   man who tried so desperately to understand anything all
12   his life, through wide eyes and a quarter smile. Do you
13   know that look? No smile big enough to cause dimples,
14   nothing big enough to leave that kind of mark. But the
15   eyes are open big and the forehead's made to suffer with
16   a few crinkles. Yes, that look. The one that looks like
17   you're trying and you know you're trying. That's the look
18   you're giving me now.

Barriers
by Michael Kearns

1   *In* Life Expectancies, *Louise, a kind-hearted and mature*
2   *mental health professional, does volunteer work with the*
3   *mentally ill population on Los Angeles' skid row. She is a*
4   *beacon of light to those wretched souls who have descended*
5   *into the maelstrom of big-city degradation. Set against this*
6   *drab skyline, Louise paints a grim-faced portrait of Joey, one*
7   *of her patients who chose to hang himself after a long*
8   *romance with death.*
9
10   **LOUISE:** It seems you never really know anyone until
11   after they die. There was a leather belt around his neck,
12   intricately and skillfully looped around the pole. Only
13   later did I realize that I had made a mental note that
14   something seemed out of place about the belt. It didn't
15   match the shirts that were strewn about or the shoes he
16   was wearing. I don't mean match like in color
17   coordination. It just stood out; the belt seemed to be
18   breathing even though Joey wasn't. Does that sound
19   crazy? I'm from the old school. A nurse does everything
20   to save a life. Vomit is nothing. Nothing. Sure, it was
21   everywhere — copious amounts of vomit. On my
22   clothes. In my hair. My nose. My mouth. I wasn't
23   thinking about whether he was HIV-positive. I do
24   remember thinking that he was in his twenties, same as
25   my two boys, my sons. He looked like my oldest son. I
26   had one of those barriers in my purse — a piece of
27   plastic with a hole in it you're supposed to put over their
28   mouth during CPR. I bought one — a barrier — for six
29   bucks. Comes in a cute little pouch that was somewhere

1 in my purse. At that point, did I even know where my
2 purse was? When most people hang themselves, they do
3 it from a certain height so their feet can't touch the floor.
4 Joey was just slumped over. He had to force himself, force
5 himself to stop breathing. That's why people step off a
6 chair — so there's no turning back. Even if the mind says
7 you want to die, the body takes over. It's hard to fight the
8 body's desire to survive. In most hanging cases, when the
9 person jumps, they break their neck — that's what kills
10 them. Joey's neck wasn't broken. He strangled himself
11 with all his might. He really wanted to die. He had an
12 ongoing romance with death, finally consummated.
13   I cried most of the day on Saturday, fearing that I'd go
14 back into my own black hole. While I have no idea how it
15 feels to be homeless or locked up in prison or abandoned
16 by my family, I understood his pain. You have no idea how
17 much respect and admiration I have for them. Listen, I had
18 a certain privilege at birth — call it luck, whatever — or I
19 would be dead. They were not born lucky. I spoke to his
20 father on the phone. He was sobbing uncontrollably. There
21 were so many barriers between them — Joey's sexuality,
22 his drug use, his mental illness. His father asked if he
23 could come and get Joey's things. A television, a DVD
24 player, clothes, a few books, those Carmen Miranda
25 pictures. He asked if there was any money. There was,
26 and we gave it to him. We had gotten rid of the gay porn
27 magazines. And I didn't quite know how to explain
28 something I did. Intuitively. I took the belt. His belt. I
29 stuffed it in my purse when no one was looking.
30 Something made me. Something told me to take it. Only
31 later that evening did I realize there was dried vomit on it.
32 I cleaned it, the belt covered with Joey's dry puke and my
33 wet tears. I found a box, a pretty box, and put the clean
34 belt in it. I placed the box in a special drawer where I keep
35 all my treasures — photos of my family, cherished letters,

1   trinkets from cities I've visited. The drawer is a storehouse
2   of memories that keep me alive. That's where Joey's belt
3   belongs.

Kissing
by Robert Caisley

1   *Tess, a pert, professional woman with a strong sense of who*
2   *she is, works in the insurance business and appears on all*
3   *accounts to be focused, secure, and fantastically happy in her*
4   *profession. However, during a speech delivered at a local high*
5   *school Career Day, Tess experiences a momentary crisis of*
6   *conscience and confesses the deep sense of personal*
7   *disappointment she feels in having compromised her*
8   *childhood dream of becoming a dancer.*
9

10   **TESS: I was quiet as a child. My parents called me**
11   **"thoughtful." They were being nice. Truth was, I was**
12   **shy, painfully shy, paralyzed by it.** *(She laughs.)* **I had**
13   **this collection of hats. I'd wear them all over. Ski cap,**
14   **cowboy hat, British Bobby's hat — and I could, at a**
15   **moment's notice, when too much attention was being**
16   **paid to me — pull the brim down over my eyes. And ...**
17   **puff ... I was gone. Dad always played along.** **"*Hey*,**
18   **where did Tess go? Has anyone seen Tess?" Which is**
19   **why it came as quite a shock for everyone when I told**
20   **them what I wanted to be when I grew up.**

21   **I was eight or nine — something like that. I was**
22   **watching the news with my mother, and they came back**
23   **from a commercial and there was this image of a woman**
24   **standing in the middle of a field, in a storm. The rain**
25   **was just lashing away at her — you know, sideways —**
26   **like a hurricane or typhoon or something — and she was**
27   **saying how whole trailer parks had been lifted into the**
28   **air and thrown like children's building blocks into the**
29   **neighboring county. She's having to scream this, of**

1   course, due to the gale-force winds ... and there were
2   shots of people boarding up their homes ... and then this
3   computer graphic of a map — a meteorologist map —
4   showing the raging storm offshore that was about to make
5   landfall. And they kept cutting back to this reporter in the
6   field — literally being pummeled by the storm — her hair
7   — you know?

8   And I started screaming. At the television. Kinda
9   looney, I know, but I screamed, "Get out of there! Why are
10   you just standing there — helpless! — the middle of the
11   field? Can't you see what's coming your way? Can't you
12   sense the imminent danger?" Of course I didn't have such
13   a developed vocabulary back then. "Run," I screamed, "Or
14   you'll be sucked into the sky, and they won't find your
15   body for three days until some cop discovers it twisted up
16   in the power lines in the next town!"

17   I mean, I was frantic ... frantic, but ... she couldn't
18   hear me. And then I started to —

19   OK, this is the really looney part — I started to dance.
20   This mad dance. In order to save lives. I couldn't stop.
21   Isn't that funny? I have no idea why. It was — it was
22   involuntary and untamed ... and did a fantastic job of
23   really freaking out my parents ... and then ... then they
24   flashed the reporter's name on the screen in cobalt blue:
25   "Kathryn Doolan, Eyewitness News."

26   Reporting "live" from some weather-beaten corner of
27   the country. Live. That word ... just the idea of it ... it just
28   reverberated. To this day, if I close my eyes, I can still see
29   that little pinprick of light on our old TV set when you'd
30   shut it off. Like an afterthought. It would last for several
31   seconds — this beautiful, penetrating, lingering spot of
32   white in an ocean of darkness. And then, it was gone.
33   *(Pause. She looks around at the faces in the crowd.)*

34   Some of you will go into business. Some will become
35   doctors or lawyers or you'll work with children, maybe

1   you'll teach. You want to serve your country, become a
2   professional athlete, something. So many choices. You
3   check this little box on a form in your guidance counselor's
4   office ... check ... real estate agent ... check ... E.R.
5   nurse ... and your life starts along a certain path.

6   But — I'm sorry, I get so easily derailed — to get to the
7   original question from the girl in the back, "Why the
8   insurance business?" Well, I think, in a nutshell ... there
9   wasn't any little box to check off that said "dancer." Or
10   maybe — I'm stripping away the mask here — maybe I
11   didn't want to upset the natural balance of the universe.
12   You know because that's ... that's what I thought must
13   have happened to all those people caught in that storm.
14   They must have — they must have challenged the
15   natural ... you know? ... and this was the punishment for
16   their defiance.

17   Anyway. I'm a people person. I love giving peace of
18   mind. That's the insurance business. That's what I do.

Voices from September 11th
by Lavonne Mueller

1 *Fala, pet dog and beloved companion of President Franklin*
2 *Delano Roosevelt, voices the anguish, courage, and valor of*
3 *the heroic "war dogs" who served with distinction during the*
4 *heart-rending September 11th nightmare. The actor playing*
5 *Fala, dressed in a black bodysuit with black Scottie ears and*
6 *wearing a World War II Navy cape and grasping a cigarette*
7 *holder, gives a faithful account of canine self-sacrifice in the*
8 *face of impending death.*
9
10 FALA: Name's Fala — Franklin D. Roosevelt's dog. I
11 was sleeping by this very wheelchair when Franklin took
12 the call about Pearl Harbor. He was drinking tea and
13 dropped the cup on the floor. He stared at all those
14 splinters of glass like it was his country that had just
15 broken apart. Then he leaned over wanting to put back
16 the pieces, but of course that was impossible. There
17 was even a canvas chute outside my FDR's bedroom
18 window so he could slide down to the lawn in case of
19 fire.
20   We were just as frightened and confused as you
21 folks are right now. But sometimes I think people tend
22 to panic more than dogs do. Like I heard there's a move
23 today to change the name of the Afghan Hound Club of
24 America due to the war in Afghanistan. Luckily, the club
25 refused. Afghan Hounds are by nature pacifists.
26   Don't look too startled ... like you're seeing a ghost.
27 You all seem to think the dead sit around on clouds up
28 in heaven. Well, I'm here to tell you that's not true —
29 maybe for people, but not for dogs. I've never left

1   America. I'm still everywhere in the streets. To be dead is
2   to be more alive in a hundred thousand different ways;
3   ways that were dead to you when you were alive, like
4   having eyes that hear and think and ears that see and
5   speak.
6   My brothers are true heroes — right there at Ground
7   Zero on September eleventh. There was this blind man at
8   his desk on the seventy-eighth floor of the World Trade
9   Center. His dog, Roselle, led him and his colleagues down
10   to the first floor. As Tower Two collapsed, Roselle
11   continued to lead her companion and a trail of co-workers
12   all the way to the river and safety.
13   My kind worked side by side with all the first
14   responders at the site — like Porkchop, a two-year-old
15   Australian Shepherd who wore bandages and leather
16   booties to protect his feet. Porkchop worked a twelve-hour
17   shift, sniffing and rummaging around in the rubble. At first
18   he discovered survivors ... then he unearthed clothing or
19   personal papers, and then ... human remains. A dog's
20   eyes are just as sensitive as yours, and Porkchop and his
21   buddies' eyes were constantly burning from all the acrid
22   dust and methane gas bubbling up from the mud.
23   Sometimes they limped from getting their legs or paws
24   crimped in all the debris. Those mutts worked without
25   surgical masks and were gagged by smoke and ash
26   inhalation.
27   I don't mean to belittle the human race, but it's pure
28   fact that we dogs can smell better than any of you. That's
29   why we're so valuable. Our nose makes up a large
30   percentage of our brain space. We got two hundred and
31   thirty million scent receptors, and you folks have only ten
32   million.
33   I hate to brag, but dogs work on Pavlovian
34   conditioning, a kind of classy psychology that some of you
35   who went to college might know about. We are trained to

1   associate specific odors with a reward. If we smell a
2   briefcase under bricks and steel, for example, we know
3   we're going to get a treat from our owner.
4   Added to the horror of what happened at the Twin
5   Towers, we heard that the Taliban experimented with nerve
6   gas on us dogs. Psychologists say that notorious killers
7   often vent their fury on animals. That made rescue canines
8   even more eager to do their job.
9   Within hours of the tragedy, canines were there and
10 sniffing out many of the wounded, even as glass and steel
11 sliced into their paws. A couple of my brothers nearly
12 smothered after falling into a quicksand of ash. Many got
13 cuts on their bellies and backs from snaking through hot
14 twisted steel. A special MASH Unit for dogs, a forty-foot
15 long bus with operating room and X-ray equipment, was
16 set up at Ground Zero. Heroes, all of the Ground Zero
17 dogs: Cowboy, a Border Collie; Nero, a German Shepherd;
18 Gus, a yellow Lab from Tennessee; Bella, a Border Collie
19 from L.A.; and so many more. The Westminster Kennel
20 Club Dog Show gave the Nine-Eleven canines a special
21 salute ... and when they padded into Madison Square
22 Garden with their handlers, there was a standing human
23 ovation.
24   I'll be the first to say that a lot of non-canines put their
25 lives on the line to save pets trapped in buildings left
26 behind because of immediate evacuations. A teacher at
27 Trinity Preschool helped save the school rabbit and
28 mascot, Peter. And a human from the ASPCA climbed
29 thirty-eight stories, broke down a door, and hacked his
30 way through rubble to retrieve a gecko. He also liberated a
31 snake on the twenty-seventh floor.
32   My kind suffered stress as bad as humans did. When
33 they couldn't find anybody, they began to whine and
34 scratch themselves restlessly. Their trainers had to
35 provide exercises to help relieve the frustration and

1   anxiety over their defeat of not saving lives. One of my
2   brothers went wildly happy on discovering a man in some
3   mud bubbles. Sadly, it wasn't a real man but a bronze
4   figure by Rodin called *The Three Shades* that once stood in
5   the offices of Cantor Fitzgerald at the World Trade Center's
6   North Tower. The sculpture, now headless and footless,
7   was taken off to a landfill on Staten Island, and my brother
8   had to cope with his depression. He was trained to find the
9   living — not cadavers and statues. The Ralston Purina
10   Company, I'm happy to say, is funding a hundred-
11   thousand-dollar, three-year study to research distress
12   suffered by search and rescue dogs at the site.
13   My brothers also did therapy for people who lost loved
14   ones. Therapy dogs help grieving people. Petting an animal
15   can bring down your blood pressure.
16   *(A beat.)* I'm not particularly partial to cats, but I have
17   to admire a lady named Cleo, a feline who worked her tail
18   off comforting humans since September eleventh.
19   I guess that's why I've come back. Consider me a
20   historical therapy dog come to comfort you. I just want
21   you to know that we went through really terrible times in
22   the past. And we made it.

The Monkeyhouse
by Ryan Hughes

1   *Crystal, a serious-minded but fun-loving teen, has already*
2   *faced several obstacles in her young life that have proved to*
3   *be invaluable lessons in self preservation and survival.*
4   *Whether contorting herself in agony and pain for ballet class*
5   *or confronting an emotional relationship with her girlfriend,*
6   *Crystal has been able to deftly swerve and avoid each bump*
7   *in the road with a confident smile and a sure hand.*
8
9   **CRYSTAL: I think it's a question of how much can you**
10   **take. Like in ballet. I was in ballet for like eight years.**
11   **And the teacher was this old, old woman who couldn't**
12   **even dance, her spine was all twisted out of whack, like**
13   **this.** *(She contorts herself briefly.)* **I guess she used to be**
14   **beautiful, and she was** *this close* **to being famous, and**
15   **some disorder or something started messing with her**
16   **spine and it twisted her all around and made her**
17   **useless. Useless was** *her* **word. She said if I was gonna**
18   **be useless, to get out of her class, because she hated**
19   **all useless people, including herself, that the useless are**
20   **what the useful feed their dogs for treats. She wouldn't**
21   **call us ballerinas, we were just "girls." When I was**
22   **seven she screamed in my face.**
23   *(Contorts again.)* **"You are not a** *real ballerina* **until**
24   **you bleed through your pointe shoes!" And pointe shoes**
25   **are** *so* **hard to bleed through. But I tried. I walked**
26   **around at home en pointe. I scraped, grinded my toes**
27   **into the stiff old carpet in the basement for half an hour**
28   **before class. I cried, I was in pain, for months. One class**
29   **I was gasping and sweating and I couldn't hear the**

1   piano for the pain, and she was still *screaming* at me, my
2   toes were sticky in my shoes, I could feel them, but not
3   *enough* because the *screaming*, still, so when she looked
4   away I *kicked my toes* into the *floor!* And I was down,
5   screaming into the floor, they dragged me into a corner,
6   and the shoes were coming off, sliding away from my toes,
7   I couldn't stop screaming, *it hurt so much!* And she was
8   over me and she was smiling! She! Smiling! I was looking
9   up at everyone looking down at me and she held up the
10   bloody shoes and she said, "We have a *balle-rina!*"
11   *(A moment of suspension. She smiles, in great pain, and the*
12   *memory fades. Pause.)* I don't dance anymore. That moment
13   went away, and it never came back. When I was twelve I
14   met Angie and ballet didn't seem as important, so I quit.
15   Angie is more challenging. It's that moment again and
16   again with Angie. That moment forever. You just take it
17   all. And bleed through your shoes, and smile. I should
18   have quit sooner. Ballet, I mean.

Sanctuary
by Heidi Decker

1   *Reflecting an apocalyptic vision of the biblical Book of*
2   *Revelations, this haunting character portrait confirms the*
3   *despair of facing, wrestling, and seducing one's demons*
4   *while living the human drama. An unnamed self-seeking*
5   *woman, one of "The Grey People," is plunged into a shadowy*
6   *underworld that offers only fleeting sanctuary. There is an*
7   *impenetrable maze of mysterious circumstances here that*
8   *each of us — in our own time, perhaps — will also be forced*
9   *to confront.*
10
11   WOMAN: They call us The Grey People. From the clay.
12   There's no dirt here, on the ground. Maybe there used
13   to be, when the trees were alive, but not that I've ever
14   seen. Only this clay ... dried ... powdery ... almost like
15   soot.
16
17   It gets in your clothes, in your hair, in your mouth ... and
18   you forget what you used to look like. You forget what
19   it's like to feel clean. You forget what you look like *now*.
20   Not that it matters, really, but still.
21
22   Your self-image blurs ... the pictures you used to carry
23   inside your head fade, and streak ... as if they've been
24   soaked in water. Crumbling.
25
26   Under my fingernails, on my eyelids, between my teeth,
27   grit in my gums ... how long have we been here? I can't
28   tell anymore. Months at least. Maybe longer. I feel older,
29   but that's not much proof.

1   We've been hiding for so long ... have been cut off, for so
2   long. For all we know, the war could have ended, and a
3   new one could have started up. I don't think there is a life
4   out there anymore. I can't see it.
5
6   I think the grit is always going to be in my gums.
7
8   What's the choice? A smoldering village surrounded by
9   snipers ... or rotting in a damp cave, afraid of every
10   shadow? What's worse?
11
12   They're both hell.
13
14   Forgetting the color of your children's hair because of the
15   clay. The sky is grey, our lives are grey. Time itself is grey.
16
17   Nothing is worse than the hell of waiting.

Obesity Talks Back
by Peter Langman

1 *Abby, a spunky, passionate, painfully honest and large girl*
2 *in her late teens, stands poised and proud center stage as she*
3 *voices her deeply felt and satisfying thoughts. This is a hard-*
4 *hitting, no-punches-spared demolition of the callous and*
5 *insensitive stereotypes that crucify women who are not wafer-*
6 *thin, and is presented in vivid and startling terms.*
7
8 ABBY: Last night, I had the biggest realization of my
9 life. I suddenly realized that I am not the problem. The
10 problem isn't me or my weight or how much I eat. The
11 problem is you. The way you treat me. The way you are
12 all so hung up on weight. It's your hang-up, but I'm the
13 victim of it. Of course, you are victims, too, but that's
14 for you to figure out.
15   We're supposed to celebrate diversity, but you avoid
16 fat people like the plague. Why? Are you afraid it's
17 contagious? Maybe some fat cooties will rub off on you
18 and your life will be ruined. Are you afraid that even to
19 be seen in the vicinity of fatness diminishes your self-
20 worth or social standing? Celebrate diversity! But don't
21 let the fat people into the party. They'll eat all the food,
22 you know. Besides, what's there to celebrate about
23 them?
24   But let me ask you this — by achieving thinness,
25 does that make you smarter? Do you suddenly become
26 more talented? Does it make you a better wife? A better
27 mother? No. You know what is does make you? Afraid.
28 Afraid to eat to your heart's content. Afraid to not be
29 like everybody else. It makes you envious of women who

1   are thinner. And it makes you cruel. Cruel to people like
2   me. Cruel to your own friends, your sisters, your
3   daughters, if they happen to be plump — pudgy —
4   stocky — fat!
5   Do you really believe that thinness will bring happiness
6   and success? That thinness will protect you from all of
7   life's difficulties? Well, I've got news for you. Thin people
8   get in car accidents. It happens. Thin people get fired, laid
9   off, downsized. Thin people become alcoholics. Thin
10   people die of cancer. Thin people get dumped by their
11   boyfriends and divorced by their husbands. Yes, that
12   happens, too. Thin people even kill themselves.
13   I know, I know. You're all just dying to tell me about
14   health and how bad it is to be fat. Yeah, yeah, yeah. But
15   that's not what this is all about. If you cared about my
16   health I'd feel your concern, your sympathy, your support.
17   But you know what? That's not what I feel. All I feel is your
18   dehumanizing bigotry. And from some of you, your pity.
19   But don't get me wrong. I don't want your sympathy or
20   your pity. I don't need you to feel bad for me. If you feel
21   bad for me, that means you think you're better than I am.
22   And you're not. And you know what else? You hurt me. All
23   my life you hurt me. You told me I was ugly, and I believed
24   you. You told me I was worthless, and I believed you. You
25   told me I was unlovable, and I believed you. Well, I have
26   just one thing to say to you: You're wrong.

Viper, or A Cloud Is Not a Thing
by Stephanie Fleischmann

1   *Helen, a free-wheeling mature beauty with a good sense of*
2   *humor, is on her way to Annapolis after years away to make*
3   *amends with Rose, her fundamentalist sister. But there is a*
4   *sniper lurking on the Beltway and the threat of death looms*
5   *heavily everywhere. Helen continues on unconcerned and*
6   *provides a gripping description of how she intends to face her*
7   *destiny if the sniper should strike.*
8
9   HELEN: When I die, I want to be burned in the fires of
10 a crematorium. But I don't want my ashes standing
11 useless in an urn. And I don't want to be scattered by
12 the winds over the four corners of the earth, either. Just
13 to end up as dust on somebody's windowsill? No, uh uh.
14 I want to be cooked up so hot my ashes turn; they
15 crystallize. When I die, I wanna be a diamond. But not
16 just a ring-finger diamond. To be banged about in dirty
17 water when Janie does the dishes? No — I want to be
18 worn around her neck. On a chain so tiny it's just about
19 invisible. So I shimmer and shine every time she says a
20 word. So she remembers me every time she breathes.
21 Like I used to be. But I don't just want to be a *diamond*.
22 I want to be a pencil, too. Diamonds, graphite, they both
23 come from carbon. Graphite is an excellent conductor of
24 electricity. It's expensive, I know, but I've got just
25 enough saved, I think, to make it happen. So. There you
26 go. A diamond it is. A diamond for Janie, and there
27 should be just enough of me left over for a pencil after
28 the diamond's done. A pencil for Jimmy to write his
29 words down with: So many words he'll write with the

1   graphite pencil that is me, they'll add up to a book. He'll
2   write and write until there is no more left of me but the
3   book and a pencil stub he can put away in one of his little
4   aluminum fly-fishing boxes. Stick it in a drawer and keep
5   it for his kids when he has them — if he has them — so
6   that his kids, my grandkids, lord knows if I'm gonna live
7   to see them, rate he's going, so that my grandkids can
8   sharpen the stub, and draw stick figures and cartoons in
9   the margins of their books. With me.
10   Ask me — being made into a pencil is better than
11   going to heaven.
12   It's immortality.

WYWH
by Andrew Biss

1   *Eileen, a reclusive divorcee, surfs the net searching for*
2   *interesting sites to help her pass the time. She has a warm*
3   *and good-humored exterior that masks a lingering inner grief:*
4   *the mysterious disappearance of her seven-year old son, Billy,*
5   *who vanished ten years ago. Recalling her son's*
6   *disappearance, Eileen can only log off lovingly, "WYWH"—*
7   *wish you were here!*
8
9   EILEEN: Billy disappeared ten years ago — almost to
10 the day. He was seven years old, and I was peeling
11 potatoes. He came running into the kitchen asking for
12 money for an ice cream. I told him he could take some
13 from the jar on the counter and off he went, down to Mr.
14 Hobson's on the corner, in his little yellow sweater with
15 the hole under the arm that I never did get around to
16 mending. And that was it ... he was gone. He never did
17 make it to Mr. Hobson's. He just up and disappeared ...
18 as if by magic. *(Beat.)*
19   They searched the neighborhood with a fine-toothed
20 comb, of course. Police, friends, neighbors — they all
21 pitched in. It was all over the news, on the television, in
22 the papers. Billy's face was everywhere ... everywhere
23 except back home. Someone had put his photograph on
24 a flyer with a telephone number you could call if you had
25 any information. That flyer was posted everywhere you
26 looked. Every tree, every lamppost — you couldn't miss
27 it. But then, as time went on, his story began to
28 disappear from the news, the searches were finally
29 called off, and the flyers became faded and torn and ...

1 blew away in the wind. Everyone moved on ... everyone
2 else, that is. *(Beat.)*
3   A couple of years ago, as I was rummaging through an
4 old drawer looking for what I couldn't tell you now, I came
5 upon one of those old flyers. It gave me quite a jolt.
6 Suddenly there was Billy looking up at me ... with that
7 quizzical expression he sometimes had. I was completely
8 dumbstruck. I couldn't move. I just froze up, staring back
9 at Billy's face and the four words in big, black print written
10 underneath it that simply said, "Have you seen me?"

The Morning Bird
by Colleen Wagner

1   *Doreen, a feisty street person, has stolen an expensive*
2   *designer jacket from the hospital and waits anxiously outside*
3   *in the cold hoping to discover the owner without having to*
4   *give up the jacket. She sits on a step outside the admitting*
5   *area clutching the jacket, an unlit cigarette dangling from her*
6   *mouth. Digging her hands deep into the jacket pockets, she*
7   *pulls out a silver lighter with a flip lid. Doreen takes the*
8   *cigarette out of her mouth and uses it to point to the lighter*
9   *as she recalls her encounter with an X-ray machine.*
10
11   **DOREEN:** *(Imitating Robert DeNiro in* Taxi Driver*)* **"You**
12   **talking to me? I said, are you talking to me?"**
13   The winter is no time to get sick, I'm telling you.
14   Freeze your butt off waiting for doctors. And what do
15   they tell you — "you're pretty sick. Come back next
16   week if you're not feeling any better."
17   Sure, eh. How long you gonna do that before you get
18   the message?
19   They always take X-rays when you're sick. Those
20   doctors can't tell nothing without exposing your bones
21   to radiation. "It's safe," they say. "Less radiation than
22   you get when you're in an airplane." I don't fly. Ever. For
23   just that reason. Look what it's done to all those people
24   in Chernobyl!
25   We were told not to eat any cheese out of that part
26   of the world, but I bet lots of people are. Radiation loves
27   cheese. Anything with fat. And it stays there forever.
28   And there are those people eating all that cheese
29   thinking it's real good for them but what they don't tell

1   them is it's full of radiation which causes cancer and
2   babies to be born with two heads — *(Pulls the jacket around*
3   *her.)*
4   I love the spring. All the birds coming back. I love the
5   robins. I heard China doesn't have any birds left except the
6   ones in cages. That's because the farmers complained
7   that the birds were eating all their grain so Chairman Mao
8   told everyone to get out there and kill them. And they did.
9   And that's a lot of people — billions — going after a few
10   birds.
11   And birds don't migrate there anymore. *(Laughs.)* I
12   guess they got the message.
13   *(Remembering)* Oh yeah! X-rays! So they X-ray me.
14   They take me down to the bottom of the hospital in this
15   cold dark room that smells funny. Know that smell? The
16   smell of metal and tungsten light and they put me on a
17   metal table and twist my legs around and they shone this
18   square light on me with a black cross through it like a
19   window with four panes, and it's framing my abdomen and
20   they push a button even though I'm telling them I'm not
21   ready — and they push it anyway because nobody in the
22   basement hears me because all the metal down there has
23   made them deaf, so they push the button even though I'm
24   screaming now "*I'm not ready!*" and the table vibrates and
25   the radiation shoots through me like invisible bullets and
26   all the tiny molecules and atoms are blown to smithereens
27   because radiation does that but most of the time we don't
28   feel it unless we're sensitive and the doctors don't even
29   think about it because all they want is a good clear shot
30   of your bones but they got to get through everything else
31   to get there. Like your heart even to get through to your
32   spine!
33   I died then and there on that table. I died and woke up
34   in a hospital bed someone else.

Dear Sara Jane
by Victor Lodato

1 *It is late at night and Sara Jane, a delicate, young, angelic*
2 *woman, is seated next to a small table in her nightgown. On*
3 *the table rests a letter and a human skull. She is in a quiet,*
4 *contemplative mood, reminiscent of a Georges de la Tour*
5 *painting of Mary Magdalene. She stares intently at the skull*
6 *and then slowly turns to speak to the audience. Although*
7 *emotionally agitated, Sara Jane attempts to appear casual,*
8 *composed — even light-hearted.*
9

10 SARA JANE: I love my husband. Jerry. I love him. I do.
11 Green eyes. With little bits of copper in them. And his
12 hair, his hair is this wonderful color. Cinnamon. He's a
13 looker, Jerry. And this deep voice. It *rumbles*. Makes
14 you melt. And big beautiful hands. And they're always
15 warm. Mine are always cold. Ice. But him. Jerry. You'd
16 think he was running a fever. I'm burning up, he always
17 says. I'm burning up. In the wintertime, in bed, I put my
18 cold feet between his legs. And oh my god does he
19 curse. It's so funny. Says I'm gonna give him a heart
20 attack with those feet.
21   He must be sweating over there. 'Cause its
22 supposedly very hot there. Where he is. I worry about
23 him. It hardly seems real. All of this. I don't like to
24 watch it. On the television. I turned it on once and there
25 was this picture, this, this *image*. Oh, I mean I don't
26 even know about television in general. Lowers your
27 intelligence. And half of what you see is probably not
28 even true. Half at least. I'm not gonna let my children
29 watch it. Not too much anyway. An hour maybe if

1   they're good. Jerry and I don't have kids yet. We're gonna
2   have them though. Two or three. Jerry says two. Anyway I
3   saw this image. Children running. Foreigners you know
4   but ... they were children. And it looked like the street was
5   a river. Of blood. Some of the children were bleeding.
6   Some children were dragging other children. Trying to
7   carry them. And the screaming was like birds — like a
8   singing, like a siren. And the street like a river and I just
9   kept thinking shoes of blood. Isn't that funny?
10   *(A nervous giggle) Shoes of blood shoes of blood.* I could
11   not get that out of my head. Just spinning, you know. I
12   just get tired sometimes. Sometimes I'm walking down
13   the street and I feel like I could just lie down, right there
14   on the pavement. Last week I saw a man asleep against a
15   building. Middle of the day. Wrapped in a blanket. Not a
16   blanket, a ... a black bag, a plastic bag. And I thought to
17   myself, I could do that. Take a little nap right there on the
18   street. Isn't that funny?
19   I mean, what else was I going to do anyway? Go home
20   and no one's home. Or go to some restaurant. Meet a
21   friend for lunch. You say, *friend. Friend.* What does that
22   even mean? I mean, isn't that a funny word? The I before
23   E except after C — I always get that confused. It's not a
24   simple word. There's one side, your side, and then there's
25   them, there's the enemy. That's what this is all about. The
26   one side, your side, and then the enemy. Some of yours
27   die and some of theirs die. That's how it is in these
28   situations. I read in the newspaper about this one
29   village — it was all women and children, just like they say
30   in the movies, you know to make it very dramatic — and
31   they were all killed. They were all burned. Well, you know,
32   they say even the children are setting traps in the woods.
33   That these children, from a very early age, are taught
34   these things — how to set these horrible traps that can kill
35   a man. I'm not saying these children in this village were

1   killers. I'm not saying that. Because I know I was very
2   upset when I read about this burning of this village. I
3   talked to my mother about it. Because I was confused, I
4   was upset. But what you have to realize is that innocent
5   people always die in a war. That's what she said. She said:
6   Honey, innocent people always die in a war, that's just the
7   way it is. And that word! War. I mean, is it a war, isn't it
8   a war? They don't stop with that. I can't even say the
9   word, it's like I've got a piece of gum stuck in my mouth.
10   *War.*
11   **Oh, Jerry.** *(She looks at the skull.)*
12   **Poor Jerry.**
13   I love my husband. I love him. I do.
14   *(She quickly turns back to the audience.)* **Oh no, this**
15   isn't ... this isn't Jerry. Oh my god did you think that?
16   That's so funny. No. This is ... this is something else.
17   *(She really starts to ramble now.)* **I** don't really
18   understand the whole thing. You know. I don't get it. This
19   house, it's a beautiful house we live in. It's got a sun room.
20   There's a swing set out back. Rusty — but Jerry says he
21   can fix it up. He's an ace at cars. Fixing cars. That's what
22   he was doing before he left. But he's going back to school
23   when he comes home. Because we're just a couple of
24   miles from the community college. And we don't know
25   what yet. He's not sure. What he wants to study.
26   Restaurant management, I thought. Oh I would love to
27   open a restaurant one day. Jerry's not sure. Maybe hotel
28   management, he says. But definitely management. I
29   mean, he's got the look. And he's smart. You wouldn't
30   think it at first, but he is. He's quick, you know. And
31   funny, oh my god. His jokes. Makes everybody laugh. I
32   mean, how could a person maintain even a basic level of
33   sanity in the middle of all that? All that blood. And
34   snakes, there's snakes, you know, everywhere. And the
35   screaming, explosions. Something must happen to your

1 mind. Running around in the woods. Not the woods, what
2 do they call it ... the jungle. Jungle? Am I saying that
3 right? *Jungle.* Is that a word? I'm not gonna pretend a
4 person could maintain their what? — *manners?* —
5 maintain their manners in the middle of something like
6 that. In the middle of *jungle.* In the middle of *waaaar.* Oh,
7 you know what he could do? He could study graphic
8 design. Because he used to be really good at drawing.
9 When he was a kid. He showed me a couple of pieces. He
10 should really go back into that. I mean, he's always got
11 ideas. We have these stools in the basement, for the mini
12 bar, and they're all made from tires. Car tires. And oh my
13 god they are so comfortable. And you should see the
14 doodles he does on the phone pad. Animals and people
15 and clouds and just lines all swirled up into nothing
16 particular, but really good ...
17 *(She looks at the skull, gently touches the eye sockets.)*
18 This is where the eyes were. One here. And one here. And
19 there was a brain in here. And skin all around. Hair.
20 Tongue. Lips. He's really good with his hands, Jerry.
21 *(She is breathless for a second, turns to the side, and looks*
22 *at a wall.)* Sometimes I just watch the light moving across
23 the wall. You don't really even see it move, it sort of
24 creeps, it's like a clock. It moves when you turn away. And
25 then it's gone. Then it's dark.
26 *(With trembling hand, she picks up a letter from the table.*
27 *She stares at it and, after a moment, begins to read.)* Dear Sara
28 Jane. *That's me.* I miss you baby. I miss your body. As you
29 can see there is something in here. I am sending it home
30 for when I return. But it is for you too.
31 *(She pauses, then continues to read.)* Because we are
32 winning and we will win. I didn't kill him, he was already
33 dead. When we found him I said he was mine. Don't be
34 afraid, it's sort of a tradition. I took his head with my own
35 knife. Not easy. I boiled it down, scraped it, then boiled it

1   again. It is bleached and so it is clean, don't worry. Keep
2   it in the box or in the garage if you want. They are doing
3   things to us as well. I won't even tell you. The stars are
4   amazing here, nothing like back there. Hi to your folks and
5   your brother. Tell him I have something for him too. I'm
6   doing the best I can. I hope it is good enough. I'll be home
7   soon. Who loves you, do you know? Three guesses. Jerry.
8   Jerry. Jerry.
9   *(Her hands are visibly shaking as she lowers the letter and*
10   *she is close to tears.)* Do you know on our honeymoon we
11   stayed in a hotel that the people in the town called *la belle*
12   *du nuit.* That wasn't the real name of the hotel but it was
13   on the top of a hill and all lit up at night, so it looked very
14   beautiful from down below. When you drove up to it, in the
15   evening, you wanted to cry it was so ... it was like a place
16   you'd always been dreaming of. And you were going there.
17   *I mean, how do you ever really know another person?*
18   Really know them. I have secrets. Even from Jerry.
19   Dreams, you know. Things you'd be embarrassed to say.
20   But you know what? Because I've been thinking about
21   this. When Jerry comes home, I'm gonna tell him
22   everything. And I want him to tell me everything. I mean,
23   my god how could he ... ? Because two people should tell
24   each other — shouldn't they? — they should tell each
25   other every little thing. So there's nothing between them.
26   I just want to get everything in order, get everything
27   straight, when Jerry comes home. Because that's when
28   our life starts, doesn't it? I just wish I could fall asleep.
29   That's the thing. Just a few hours of sleep. Because you
30   don't want to get lost.
31   *(Pause.)* And it's so quiet in the house.
32   *(She looks at the skull.) And this one — this one — says*
33   *nothing.*
34   Who loves you? Do you know? Take a guess.
35   Jerry. Jerry. Jerry.

1	*(She looks at the audience and speaks through tears.)*
2	**I'm so scared.**
3	**I'm so scared.**
4	**I'm so scared.**

Marilyn: The Final Session
by Libbe S. HaLevy

1   *Marlena (Lena) Grozman, a world-renowned feminist*
2   *therapist with a prominent facial scar, encounters the*
3   *legendary film star Marilyn Monroe in an abstract Purgatory*
4   *for a therapy session. Imprisoned in limbo, neither can leave*
5   *until Lena claims her femininity and Marilyn claims her rage.*
6   *Although Marilyn rejects the fact of her death, Lena offers*
7   *ample testimony of the underlying barrenness of soul and*
8   *spirit that led her to self-destruction.*
9

10   **LENA: You ask me how I died?** *(She sings.)* **"She flies**
11   **through the air with the greatest of ... "** *Splat!*
12   **A fall from eleven stories can turn anybody into**
13   **ground round. Oh, I'm sorry, I probably shouldn't joke**
14   **about it. But it's all a joke — life, death ... this. Suicide**
15   **was supposed to be the punch line, only I'm still not**
16   **laughing. There I was, a therapy guru with a syndicated**
17   **TV program, books on the *New York Times* best-seller**
18   **list, regular gigs on *Tonight* and *Oprah*, international**
19   **seminars and a web site that sold my licensed**
20   **merchandise, everything from self-help board games to**
21   **baseball caps. In the eyes of the world, I was a complete**
22   **and total success. But I was alone, and didn't know how**
23   **to reach out or whom to reach out to for simple human**
24   **connection. I hated myself, my isolation, even my**
25   **success. I knew that all those people watching me,**
26   **applauding me, lavishing me with praise and approval —**
27   **underneath it all they felt sorry for the little girl who**
28   **would have been so pretty if only she didn't have that**
29   **horrible scar running down her face.**

1   Yes, I could have easily afforded plastic surgery. But
2   then what? Lose ten pounds, dye my hair, have a tummy
3   tuck, chin implant, liposuction, Botox? Try to please the
4   eye of others, compete for male attention — why bother? I
5   couldn't win anyway, not up against women who go into
6   hock trying to look like ... like you! *(Smiles to herself.)* I
7   learned that people trust a woman who isn't beautiful to
8   be serious about her work. *(Slowly touches scar.)* This little
9   memento pushed me further than I would have gone
10   without it. It made me a success ... Of course, it also
11   made me want to kill myself every time I looked in a
12   mirror.
13   As I grew richer and more famous, thoughts of suicide
14   became my constant companion. It felt so sensual, sitting
15   in my penthouse in the dark, night after night, sipping
16   brandy and staring out over the city lights while
17   contemplating my own demise. I often thought a suicidal
18   depression much more comforting than a skilled lover. It's
19   more intimate, more devoted, closer to the soul.
20   Flirting with death made me lust for more. One night,
21   I got up from my leather Eames chair — the one facing the
22   balcony — opened the sliding glass doors, and walked
23   outside. It was a cool night, with a little mist in the air. I
24   walked to the railing and looked over the edge. There was
25   life down there, life that was totally ignorant of my pain. I
26   hated them for not knowing how badly I felt. So I stood
27   there, looking down. And then, I sat on the railing, my feet
28   on the balcony side. Just testing myself, you know? Then
29   I swung my legs around and dangled them over the edge.
30   I didn't want to stand on the railing for fear I'd lose my
31   balance and fall by accident. One never wants these things
32   to happen by accident. So I sat there, looking down on
33   those ant-like people, feeling like the most powerful
34   woman in the world because I knew I could change their
35   lives, forever, just like that. *(Finger snap. She laughs.)*

1   I stayed there for the longest time, feeling quite serene.
2   And then, as simply as one would in a swimming pool, I
3   pushed off into the air. I'd assumed it would be all slow
4   motion and floaty ... but everything happened too fast. I
5   remember being shocked that I had actually done it. Then
6   I scrambled to take in everything. The wind, the push of
7   air against my clothes, the street noises getting louder,
8   louder. Where was I going to land? No, not on the woman
9   walking the dog! I liked dogs. Could I steer myself onto the
10   newspaper kiosk? Too late! I landed on a taxi cab, bounced
11   twice and splattered all over the *New York Times* early
12   edition. *(Pause.)*

13   Strange. There wasn't any pain. I felt a jolt, like a
14   sudden electric shock, and then my body bounced one way
15   and "I" went another. Straight up. Floating for real this
16   time, like I had expected on the way down. And I could see
17   everything — my body still twitching, blood everywhere. I
18   was grateful that you couldn't see my scar any more. But
19   then, you couldn't find my face. The lady with the dog was
20   screaming, the dog was yowling and straining at its leash,
21   and the newspaper vendor fainted. I think the taxi driver got
22   hurt. His windshield shattered when I caved in the roof. I
23   was sorry about that. People started running, yelling for an
24   ambulance, fire, police ... It didn't matter to me. I was out
25   of it ... floating ... drifting ... gone far away ... to here. *(With*
26   *a sigh, and a deep sense of irony, she sits back in her chair.)*

Amy's View
by David Hare

1   *Amy, a sensitive young woman with an unmistakable air of*
2   *vulnerability, desperately pursues hopes and dreams that*
3   *never quite live up to reality. Amy's view of life is*
4   *unconditional: You have to give yourself completely to love,*
5   *in spite of the obstacles, and one day you will be rewarded.*
6   *Here, Amy confronts her mother and defends her failing*
7   *marriage as she struggles to assert herself as an independent*
8   *woman.*
9
10 **AMY: You never saw it. Dominic was funny and gentle.**
11 **Ambitions destroyed him, that's all. Because he thinks**
12 **that the world of the media matters. He actually thinks**
13 **that it's real. So it's been harder to reach him. It's true.**
14 **So he's gone off with someone who cares about photos**
15 **in magazines, and opinion columns, and all of those dud**
16 **London things. But that doesn't mean the man was**
17 **always contemptible. It doesn't mean I shouldn't have**
18 **been with him at all. It just means ... oh look ... the**
19 **odds were against us. But I happen to think it was well**
20 **worth a try.** *(AMY's anger has turned to distress, the tears*
21 *starting to run down her cheek.)* **Of course I knew ... do**
22 **you think I'm an idiot? I always sensed: One day this**
23 **man will trade up. He'll cash me in and he'll get a new**
24 **model. I always felt it would come. These men, they**
25 **wait. They wait till they're ready. You make them secure.**
26 **Then of course when you've built the statue ... that's**
27 **when they kick the ladder away. But I did know it. I did**
28 **it knowingly. It was my choice.**

Chapter 7
Mirror Images:
Duo Scenes

> "Two friends, two bodies …
> with one soul inspired."
> — Homer, *The Illiad*

Performing duo scenes, or duologues, is a collaborative partnership that requires a healthy working relationship between two actors sharing an analysis of the text, but also taking equal turns sharing the performance spotlight. The expectations for duologues are essentially the same as you discovered in reading Chapters 1 and 2. There has to be careful attention paid to the basic principles of text analysis, the design of a performance blueprint, and a focused period of rehearsal that tunes the voice and tones the body for a stage-worthy performance. Sharing these responsibilities with another actor will need to be carefully coordinated to effectively communicate the action, attitude, and intention of *each* character appearing in the scene.

A partnership also suggests that there should be mutual collaboration on defining character business, movement, and staging the scene. Each actor may exercise individual selectivity or objectivity in an *interpretation* of the text, but there must be *consensus* on the primary character objectives and performance concept. With these thoughts in mind, you should approach the following duologues with a critical and discriminating eye. Select a partner most capable of giving subtle expression and nuance to these complex roles. Select a partner with well-rounded vocal and physical qualities. Select a partner who is agile and flexible, capable of playing both comic and serious character roles. Finally, select a partner who has the skills to engage in meaningful text analysis that will translate into an informed and imaginative performance.

The characters from these playscripts speak in many voices and make for amusing or, sometimes, wise listening. The voices here are urban or small town, sensitive or entirely unsentimental, naughty or nice, and absurd or bizarre. There are a number of half-happy endings, and several of the characters have apparently discovered a reality beyond the one in which they already live. Most appear to be temporarily lost — in either time or space — but are still holding on to their fraudulent memories, bankrupt dreams, or some gnawing divination of their own making. The characters wag their tongues to make a point, and there is general hilarity — usually at someone else's expense — and then some surprisingly bittersweet resolution of the given circumstances of the text.

In playing the scenes, work closely with your partner to ensure that there is sufficient vocal and physical contrast to clearly distinguish each character in performance. A detailed analysis blueprint for each character should provide initial clues to focus attention on the obvious *differences* in each character's age, attitude, mood, or motivation in the scene. Don't neglect, however, to consider the essential character *similarities*, and to subtly highlight them to give added dimension to a three-dimensional performance. As a rehearsal technique, improvisation of the scenes — especially vocal and physical interactions — may provide additional clues for character development. Improvisation may also reveal the moment-to-moment interpersonal relationship of the characters that is essential to an honest and truthful partnership performance.

Elephants and Coffee
by Aoise Stratford

1   *A harried woman wearing dark glasses and carrying a coffee*
2   *enters hurriedly. She is dressed conservatively, a little edgy,*
3   *and trying desperately to appear normal. She pauses at a*
4   *street corner — represented by a garbage can — nervously*
5   *looks around, then comes forward to address the audience.*
6   *Later, the elephant, a small man in a loose gray suit, enters*
7   *just as hurriedly — but quietly — and bumps into the woman.*
8   *The elephant is patient, gentle, romantic, and wise. It is a*
9   *madcap meeting, but a match! Sparks fly ... and there is*
10 *romance in the air. After a barrage of seedy insults and verbal*
11 *pratfalls, the woman makes a startling discovery: She has*
12 *met her soul-mate, who just happens to be an Elephant. Ain't*
13 *we crazy?*
14
15 **WOMAN: I know what you're thinking. I don't look like**
16 **the type. But I'm telling you that strange things happen**
17 **to ordinary people. They do. Normal people like you and**
18 **me can experience ... well, maybe it's fate. Maybe it's**
19 **some weird cosmic thing.** *(A beat.)*
20 **You don't believe me. I suppose I can understand**
21 **that. I'm still getting used to it myself. But I'm telling**
22 **you, last Saturday was without a doubt, the strangest**
23 **Saturday morning I ever had. Well, except for the**
24 **Saturday morning about three years ago when two**
25 **giraffes in wrap-around sunglasses came and stole my**
26 **husband away through the kitchen window. But really,**
27 **you've never seen anything like this elephant. I was on**
28 **my way to an appointment with my therapist.** *(A beat.)*
29 **Well, there's no need to look at me like that, half the**

1 country is on Prozac or going quietly mad in their
2 bedrooms. Hey, anyone not in therapy is crazy. But as I
3 say, I was on my way to see my therapist ... and my
4 therapist makes me nervous. Coffee calms me, so I
5 stepped into Starbucks. I ordered a grande triple shot, and
6 I left. Then it happened. Elephants, contrary to popular
7 belief, move quickly and quietly. And they don't have good
8 eyesight. I was waiting at the crosswalk when suddenly ...
9 *(Enter the ELEPHANT, a small man in a loose gray suit. He*
10 *crosses quickly but quietly and bumps into the WOMAN.)*
11 ELEPHANT: Oh my goodness! I am sorry.
12 WOMAN: *(To audience)* He didn't see me.
13 ELEPHANT: I didn't see you.
14 WOMAN: *(To audience)* At first, I didn't see him either. He
15 was quite small. Some people may have mistaken him for
16 a small man in a loose gray suit.
17 ELEPHANT: *(To audience)* It was just like she said. I wasn't
18 looking where I was going. Or she wasn't looking where
19 she was standing. And as luck would have it, I bumped
20 into her.
21 WOMAN: *(To audience)* Swept me off my feet.
22 ELEPHANT: I'm sorry. I spilled your coffee. How
23 embarrassing ... please forgive me.
24 WOMAN: I most certainly will not, you clumsy ...
25 ELEPHANT: Yes?
26 WOMAN: Oh, my. You're ...
27 ELEPHANT: An elephant?
28 WOMAN: Yes!
29 ELEPHANT: And you're a monkey!
30 WOMAN: No.
31 ELEPHANT: A primate?
32 WOMAN: A woman.
33 ELEPHANT: *(Excited, gesturing wildly with one arm)* You
34 wouldn't believe what trouble that gets me into!
35 Primates! I mean, women!

1 WOMAN: *(To audience)* Something in the way he moved ...
2 moved me. Perhaps it would be fair to say I've always had
3 a bit of a thing for elephants. You see, six months before
4 he was taken off by the giraffes, my husband and I went
5 on vacation to Botswana. A safari. We were trying to save
6 our marriage. Getting in touch with nature, with our
7 natures. We went out one morning to see the elephants.
8 Up at dawn, dressed in khaki, a boat load of us with our
9 zoom lenses and bottled water. And there they were.
10 Elephants. Everywhere. And the thing that struck me
11 about them was that they looked like they were trying so
12 hard to fit in with their surroundings. Nonchalantly
13 picking up foliage with their enormous noses, pretending
14 like that was normal.
15 ELEPHANT: Well, there's normal, and then there's normal.
16 If you had my nose ... Never mind.
17 WOMAN: *(To audience)* My husband and I sat in the jeep and
18 watched them, quietly thrilled, quietly terrified. And all
19 the while they were just too big. Too obvious. There was
20 something quietly desperate about them. Despite their
21 silly noses. I respected that. *(A beat.)* My husband liked
22 the lions. But what would you expect?
23 ELEPHANT: Can I buy you a ... what is it you're drinking?
24 WOMAN: Coffee. Grande triple latte. With a shot of vodka.
25 ELEPHANT: Vodka? Oh dear. That's not good, not good at
26 all. I had vodka once. Back when I lived at the zoo. Some
27 kids gave it to me in one of those little paper cups the
28 peanuts sometimes came in. It was awful.
29 WOMAN: I'm sorry.
30 ELEPHANT: I got the cup stuck on one of my tusks. It was
31 very embarrassing. I got quite upset and they had to give
32 me tranquilizers.
33 WOMAN: Tranquilizers? Really? Awesome!
34 ELEPHANT: It made me feel ... well, you know what I mean,
35 don't you?

1   WOMAN: No, I ... I don't take tranquilizers. Not really. And
2   I only take a little vodka. Just a nip. In my coffee. And
3   not every morning. But today I just felt like I needed ...
4   well, never mind.
5   ELEPHANT: At least let me try and fix the damage. *(He*
6   *awkwardly tries to pat her down; she brushes him away.)*
7   WOMAN: Where were you going, anyway?
8   ELEPHANT: The circus.
9   WOMAN: *(To the audience, ironic)* So suddenly, we had
10   something in common.

Aw, Shucks!
by Edward Crosby Wells

1   *At first glance, this short but compact scene appears to follow*
2   *a typical pattern made popular by theatre of the absurd*
3   *comedies. A familiar everyday event is used to focus attention*
4   *on simple and unassuming characters who seem to be lost or*
5   *incapable of understanding their present situation. As a*
6   *consequence of their disorientation, the characters are also*
7   *unable to communicate with each other in easily understood*
8   *language. The setting here is a bus stop where two solitary*
9   *figures, Eddie and Susie, pass a brief period of time posing*
10   *intriguing questions to each other and then answering them*
11   *with equally puzzling responses. They gallop along with*
12   *comic ease, skewering logic and reason, while we are left to*
13   *make sense of their apparent nonsense.*
14
15   **EDDIE:** Howdy, Susie.
16   **SUSIE:** Howdy right back atcha, Eddie.
17   **EDDIE:** So where ya'll headed?
18   **SUSIE:** Yonder.
19   **EDDIE:** I 'spects I ain't never been to Yonder.
20   **SUSIE:** Gots me a cousin up in Yonder.
21   **EDDIE:** Really? I gots me one down Nowhere.
22   **SUSIE:** I've been to Nowhere. Couldn't wait to get out and
23   get to Somewhere.
24   **EDDIE:** That's where most o' my folks live. Nice place.
25   **SUSIE:** Yep.
26   **EDDIE:** Yep. I was born and raised in Somewhere. Were
27   you always from Here?
28   **SUSIE:** Nope. I moved to Here from Yonder.
29   **EDDIE:** Yonder's nice.

1 SUSIE: Yep.

2 EDDIE: Yep.

3 SUSIE: I like Hither better. Got an uncle in Hither.

4 EDDIE: I gots me an aunt in Hither. Here it is. There's m'
5   bus.

6 SUSIE: Yep. There it is.

7 EDDIE: Yep.

8 SUSIE: Mine too.

9 EDDIE: Really?

10 SUSIE: Only I'm goin' in the opposite direction.

11 EDDIE: Then you best be gettin' on first.

Boy Meets Girl
by Wendy Wasserstein

1   *Dan and Molly are two single and successful New York City*
2   *sophisticates who have a paranoid fear of commitment. Each,*
3   *with the long-term help of their psychiatrists, has been*
4   *struggling to break free from this self-destructive web that*
5   *strangles any potential long-term relationship. On a humid*
6   *night in late August, Dan slips into the Trading Post — a*
7   *popular late-night singles' watering hole — and it's here that*
8   *he first sees Molly, seated alone at the bar. He knows*
9   *immediately that Molly is the kind of new-fashioned girl he*
10   *could bring home to his analyst's couch ... so he sits next to*
11   *her and opens the conversation with his best pick-up lines.*
12
13   DAN: Hi.
14   MOLLY: Hi.
15   DAN: Do you come here often?
16   MOLLY: Never.
17   DAN: I don't either.
18   MOLLY: I'm waiting here for a friend. She selected this
19   place. I think what's happening to the West Side is
20   outrageous.
21   DAN: This is really an East Side singles kind of
22   restaurant.
23   MOLLY: Yes, but it's here on the West Side, so we have to
24   deal with it.
25   DAN: You sound like a concerned citizen.
26   MOLLY: Did you ever read any Kenneth Burke? In college,
27   maybe? Lit. Crit.?
28   DAN: *(Immediately)* Oh, sure.
29   MOLLY: He divides people into observers, spectators, and

1 participants. I'm here strictly as a sociological observer.
2 I love to watch people in New York. Otherwise I would
3 never come to a place like this.
4 DAN: I wouldn't either. In my spare time I write film
5 criticism.
6 MOLLY: *(More interested)* Oh, you're a critic! Who do you
7 write for?
8 DAN: I write for myself. I keep a film criticism journal.
9 MOLLY: I love film. Women in film particularly interest me.
10 My favorites are Diane Kurys, Doris Dorrie, and Lee
11 Grant.
12 DAN: I love women in film too.
13 MOLLY: *(Impressed)* You're so direct and forthcoming. What
14 do you do?
15 DAN: I'm a psychiatrist.
16 MOLLY: Individual, group, house calls?
17 DAN: Actually, I'm a creative director at the B.B.D.&O.
18 advertising agency. But I think of it as psychology.
19 Dealing with the individual's everyday dreams and
20 desires. I'm in charge of the Scott Paper account.
21 MOLLY: Fascinating. I use tissues a lot. I've always
22 wondered why.
23 DAN: What do *you* do?
24 MOLLY: I'm a systems analyst for American Express.
25 DAN: "Do you know me?"
26 MOLLY: *(Very straightforward)* Not very well. But I'd like to.
27 DAN: *(Looks at her intently.)* Why don't we go somewhere a
28 little less trendy to talk. I can tell these aren't your kind
29 of people.
30 MOLLY: No, I don't belong here. This isn't my New York.
31 DAN: *(Helps her with her coat.)* That's a nice jacket.
32 MOLLY: Donna Karan. But I've moved on to Issey Miyake.
33 DAN: *(Putting on a multi-layered karate jacket)* We have so
34 much in common.
35 MOLLY: "It's a phenomenon." That's a quote from a song in

1   *Gypsy,* "Small World, Isn't It?" I love Stephen Sondheim.
2   DAN: I'm afraid I don't know much about theatre. I'm a
3   workaholic. You know, mid-thirties New York guy, longing
4   for Real Relationship with Remarkable Woman,
5   meanwhile finds fulfillment through his work.
6   MOLLY: I think I like you. But be careful, I have Fear of
7   Intimacy.
8   DAN: The Bachelor Girl's Disease. I hear it's an epidemic.
9   MOLLY: I'm working with my shrink to get past it. *(Pause as*
10   *Dan looks at her.)*
11   DAN: I think I like you, too. *(They begin to exit restaurant.)*
12   What about your girlfriend?
13   MOLLY: Uh, ah, she told me if she wasn't here by now she
14   wasn't coming.
15   DAN: Not a very reliable friend.
16   MOLLY: No, but she's working with her shrink to get past it.
17   *(They exit.)*

Stolen Identity
by Steve Ghent

1   *In this original duologue, a rather smart and good-natured*
2   *woman who is on a run of bad luck has recently had her*
3   *identity stolen and unexpectedly comes face-to-face with the*
4   *culprit in a head-on comic collision. The two wise-cracking*
5   *warriors circle each other and verbally spar with surprising*
6   *suspense and reversals galore. What follows is a royal battle*
7   *to sort out who is the real victim here! The keen-witted,*
8   *shrewd culprit is unrepentant and even indignant at what*
9   *she considers to be an attack on her personal character, and*
10   *recounts the humiliating mishaps that have resulted since*
11   *she assumed such a "worthless" identity. The perpetual*
12   *plaintiff struggles to put up a good front but quickly realizes*
13   *that she will have her hands full trying to unravel this*
14   *mystery and reclaim her true identity.*
15
16   **WOMAN** 1: *(Running, anxious)* **Ms. Roberta Duggin! Ms.**
17   **Duggin! Are you Roberta Duggin?**
18   **WOMAN 2:** *(Laid-back)* **Well, yes.**
19   **WOMAN 1: Ah-ha! I caught you. The counter attendant**
20   **told me "I" just tried to purchase a ticket, two people**
21   **before me. I'm the *real* Ms. Roberta Duggin. You've**
22   **stolen my identity for the last time. What do you have**
23   **to say for yourself?**
24   **WOMAN 2: OK, OK, you caught me. I admit it. Actually,**
25   **you should feel bad for me.**
26   **WOMAN 1: What?**
27   **WOMAN 2: Your credit stinks. Do you know how embarrassing**
28   **that was to be turned down for credit in front of all those**
29   **people? I was humiliated for you. You should be so**

1   flattered I even wanted to use your card.

2   WOMAN 1: You stole my identity!

3   WOMAN 2: What identity? You're the reason crossword

4   puzzles exist. I've realized there are millions of

5   Americans out there with so-called identities like yourself

6   that have no life.

7   WOMAN 1: It's because of you I wasn't able to get my car

8   loan to go through.

9   WOMAN 2: You couldn't have anyway. You were sixty days

10   late on the expensive new furniture last November. Ever

11   heard of Goodwill? Then all the credit inquiries — that

12   lowered your score even more. You're worthless! Inquiries

13   make the card companies think you're desperate.

14   WOMAN 1: I was! The inquiries were to get a new card

15   because the old one was frozen. Took sixty days to get

16   reimbursed and I still had to pay a fifty-dollar fee. *(Beat.)*

17   Worthless?

18   WOMAN 2: Yes, I'm sorry to tell you. I wouldn't want to be

19   caught dead with your credit.

20   WOMAN 1: I have kids to support. And kids *have* to have

21   the best shoes.

22   WOMAN 2: Yeah, they do. Look, I'm a mother, too. *(Pulls out*

23   *money.)* I'm going to give you the fifty dollars back. Never

24   let it be said I don't have a heart. Anyways, I'm late for

25   your flight.

26   WOMAN 1: You said they turned my Visa down.

27   WOMAN 2: They did. Then I had to use a MasterCard. See

28   ya. *(Walks away.)*

29   WOMAN 1: *(Looks at money. Beat.)* Cash! From my MasterCard!

The Last Yankee
by Arthur Miller

1   *Karen Frick and Patricia Alexander, two mature women from*
2   *prosperous backgrounds, have become close friends and*
3   *confidants. They are roommates at a private hospital, each*
4   *recovering from a nervous breakdown, and share an*
5   *overwhelming sense of despair and depression. Although*
6   *quiet and unassuming on the outside, both are self-imploding*
7   *beneath the surface. Patricia cannot reconcile her husband's*
8   *apparent lack of initiative and underachievement. She has*
9   *refused anti-depression medicine for several weeks, and now*
10   *exhibits more clarity in her thoughts. Karen shares an equally*
11   *strained marriage with a distant husband, but has been*
12   *slower to show signs of recovery and is still confused at*
13   *times. They have been sharing stories about their spouses*
14   *and, in a final session before joining their husbands in the*
15   *waiting room, have one more moment of connection before*
16   *the captives meet their captors.*

17

18   KAREN: I feel so ashamed.

19   PATRICIA: For heaven's sake, why? You've got a right to
20   be depressed. There's more people in hospitals
21   because of depression than any other disease.

22   KAREN: Is that true?

23   PATRICIA: Of course! Anybody with any sense has got to
24   be depressed in this country. Unless you're really rich,
25   I suppose. Don't let him shame you, dear.

26   KAREN: No ... it's that you have so many thoughts.

27   PATRICIA: Oh. Well, you can have thoughts, too — just
28   remember your soul belongs to God and you mustn't
29   be shoving pills into his mouth.

1   *(Slight pause.)*
2 KAREN: We're rich, I think.
3 PATRICIA: *(Quickly, interested)* ... Really rich?
4 KAREN: He's got the oil delivery now, and of course, he
5   always had the fertilizer and the Chevy dealership, and of
6   course the lumber yard and all. And Isuzu's now.
7 PATRICIA: What's Isuzu?
8 Karen: It's a Japanese car.
9 PATRICIA: ... I'll just never catch up.
10 KAREN: We go to Arkansas in the spring.
11 PATRICIA: Arkansas?
12 KAREN: For the catfish. It's where I broke down. But I can't
13   help it, the sight of catfish makes me want to vomit. Not
14   that I was trying to ... you know ... do anything. I just
15   read the instructions on the bottle wrong. Do you mind if
16   I ask you something?
17 PATRICIA: I hope it's nothing personal, is it?
18 KAREN: Well, I don't know.
19 PATRICIA: ... Well, go ahead, what is it?
20 KAREN: Do you shop in the A&P or Stop & Shop?
21 PATRICIA: ... I'm wondering if you've got the wrong
22   medication. But I guess you'll never overdose — you
23   vomit at the drop of a hat. It may be your secret blessing.
24 KAREN: He wants to get me out of the house more, but it's
25   hard to make up my mind where.
26 PATRICIA: Well ... A&P is good. Or Stop & Shop. More or
27   less. Krogers is good for fish sometimes.
28 KAREN: Which do you like best? I'll go where you go.
29 PATRICIA: You're very flattering. *(Stands, inner excitement)*
30   It's amazing — I'm really beginning to feel wonderful,
31   maybe I ought to go home with him today. I mean what
32   does it come down to, really? — it's simply a question of
33   confidence ...
34 KAREN: I wish we could raise some vegetables like we did
35   on the farm. Do you?

1 PATRICIA: Oh, he raises things in our yard. Healthy things
2   like salsify and collards — and kale. You ever eat kale?
3 KAREN: I can't remember kale.
4 PATRICIA: You might as well salt your shower curtain and
5   chop it up with a tomato.
6 KAREN: So ... meats are ... which — A&P?
7 PATRICIA: No. Meats are Stop & Shop. I'm really thinking I
8   might go home today. It's just not his fault. I have to
9   remember that ...
10 KAREN: But staples?
11 PATRICIA: What? — Oh, Stop & Shop.
12 KAREN: Then what's A&P for?
13 PATRICIA: Vegetables.
14 KAREN: Oh right. And Krogers?
15 PATRICIA: Why don't you just forget Krogers.
16 KAREN: *(Holds up five fingers, bends one at a time.)* Then Stop
17   & Shop ...
18 PATRICIA: Maybe it's that you're trying to remember three
19   things. Whyn't you just do A&P and Stop & Shop?
20   *(Slight Pause.)*
21 KAREN: I kind of liked Krogers.
22 PATRICIA: Then go to Krogers, for heaven's sake!
23 KAREN: Well, I guess I'll go out to him. *(Moves to go. Halts.)*
24   I hope you aren't really leaving today, are you?
25 PATRICIA: *(Higher tension)* I'm deciding.
26 KAREN: Well ... here I go, I guess. *(Halts again.)* I meant to
27   tell you, I kind of like the banjo. It's very good with tap
28   dancing.
29 PATRICIA: Tap dancing.
30 KAREN: There's a tap teacher lives on our road.
31 PATRICIA: You tap dance?
32 KAREN: Well, John rented a video of Ginger Rogers and
33   Fred Astaire, and I kind of liked it. I can sing "Cheek to
34   Cheek"? Would you like to hear it?
35 PATRICIA: Sure, go ahead — this is certainly a surprise.

1 KAREN: *(Sings in a frail voice.)* "Heaven, I'm in heaven, and
2   the cares that clung around me through the week ..."
3 PATRICIA: That's beautiful, Karen! Listen, what exactly
4   does Doctor Rockwell say about you?
5 KAREN: Well, he says it's quite common when a woman is
6   home alone all day.
7 PATRICIA: What's common?
8 KAREN: Someone moving around in the next room?
9 PATRICIA: Oh, I see. — You have any idea who it is?
10 KAREN: My mother. — My husband might bring my tap
11   shoes and tails ... but he probably forgot. I have a high
12   hat and shorts too. And a walking stick. But would they
13   allow dancing in here?
14 PATRICIA: They might. But of course the minute they see
15   you enjoying yourself they'll probably try to knock you
16   out with a pill.

Frailty, Thy Name Is Woe
by Paddy Gillard Bentley

1   *In this off-key, side-bar parody of Shakespeare's graveyard*
2   *scene in* Hamlet, *the more seasoned Hamlet's Father's Ghost*
3   *and the newly-deceased neophyte spectre of Ophelia meet*
4   *and debate an intriguing question: Which has more influence*
5   *in death, love or revenge? Hamlet's father, crisply dramatic*
6   *and vengeful to a fault, is intently watching the "invisible"*
7   *graveyard scene from Act V, scene i. (This parody scene takes*
8   *place at the same time, but before Hamlet and Horatio,*
9   *Ophelia's brother, enter and fight over her open grave.) An*
10 *ideal spectator, the ghost of Hamlet's father applauds to see*
11 *that his son's noblest impulses have been stirred into action*
12 *at last. Enter the mad Ophelia, dripping wet, still in love with*
13 *Hamlet but verging on collapse. She is a slow-moving,*
14 *graphic panorama of unrelieved woe, and looks a little*
15 *bewildered. Their exchanges echo familiar passages in*
16 Hamlet *and vibrate with sizzling satire.*
17
18 OPHELIA: Am I? Or not?
19 GHOST: Ah, Ophelia ... a curious question. What was it
20   he said? Within the madness of the mind to suffer the
21   slings and arrows of outrageous ...
22 OPHELIA: Love! Or to embrace a passion verily
23   unrequited.
24 GHOST: Ah, there's the rub. Look, there comes your love
25   now. *(OPHELIA begins to go to Hamlet, but the GHOST*
26   *grabs her arm.)* You will seem to my son to be of more
27   translucent substance than a whispered breeze.
28 OPHELIA: But he could see you! He did swear upon his
29   own heart he spoke with you.

1   GHOST: My intention is more essential than is thine.

2   OPHELIA: But I ...

3   GHOST: *(Monotonous)* Yes, I know ... when love speaks, the

4   voice of all the gods makes heaven drowsy with the

5   harmony ... et cetera, et cetera, et cetera. *(Vibrant)* Love's

6   influence and qualities are inferior to that of vengeance.

7   OPHELIA: I hoped, perchance he'd dream of me. But in my

8   sleep of death, what dreams may come staring at love's

9   eternal sky from beneath yon icy river?

10   GHOST: Good Gods, Ophelia. Frailty, thy name is woe ...

11   OPHELIA: Do not ... make blithe of my anguish! Look! His

12   deportment is that of a man who has lost naught. Or is

13   it his madness that precludes even one equivocal tear

14   shed for mine own providence?

15   GHOST: Vengeance hath more power in death, than has

16   love. I persuaded Hamlet to swear revenge on this foul

17   and most unnatural murder and as consequence, make

18   public the veracity of my ... yes ... brother. His mind is

19   consumed with retribution ... not of you.

20   OPHELIA: But his love for me had ...

21   GHOST: Apparently been diminished by something more

22   fervent.

23   OPHELIA: So then ...

24   GHOST: Yes.

25   OPHELIA: And I ...

26   GHOST: Uh huh.

27   OPHELIA: Oh ye tempest that is the rage of winter's wrath,

28   be not true to the heart of love. Why come through ye the

29   palest fragile blooms of spring, that we may breathe the

30   air of hope, and be cleansed by the warmest breezes of

31   May? Not even the dread of nothing subsequent to death,

32   dissuaded my will naught, for I feared his sentiment for

33   me had been vanquished by his insanity, not merely by

34   his fading devotion. I dreamed I could touch him in death,

35   I believed with ...

1   **GHOST: He pledged me his vengeance!**
2   **OPHELIA: He pledged me his love!** *(As she trudges to the exit)*
3   **Sweet breath no more uttering his name in sacred tryst.**
4   **Neither revenge ... nor my skin turned blue from sorrow**
5   **will circumscribe his wretched solitude.** *(OPHELIA exits.*
6   *HAMLET'S FATHER'S GHOST laughs.)*
7   **GHOST: Silly girl, Hamlet knows not she has died.** *(A glance*
8   *over)* **Ah, now he does.** *(Beat)* **Well, I believe, in this state**
9   **of affairs, but for the taking of my brother's life ... the**
10   **violence is ended.** *(As he moves to the exit)* **I am in no**
11   **doubt.** *(He stops.)* **You know, to be run through by an**
12   **adversary's sword is the uncomplicated way to give up**
13   **the ghost.**

The Underpants
by Carl Sternheim; adapted by Steve Martin

1   *Steve Martin, the well-known comic film actor, has adapted*
2   *Carl Sternheim's classic farce,* The Underpants, *and the*
3   *hilarious result is a laugh riot of off-the-wall humor,*
4   *suggestive word play, and wild satire. The storyline revolves*
5   *around Louise and Theo Markes, a married couple whose*
6   *ultra-conservative and rigid lifestyle is suddenly shattered*
7   *when Louise inadvertently allows her underpants to fall to*
8   *the ground during a public parade for the king. Although*
9   *Theo fears that he and his wife will be financially ruined and*
10   *become social outcasts from the inevitable scandal, he is not*
11   *prepared for the fast-paced action that follows. Louise's*
12   *momentary public display attracts two infatuated men, each*
13   *of whom now wish to rent the spare room in the Markes'*
14   *house — and are willing to pay any price — in order to be*
15   *closer to the object of their affection. In this scene, Versati, a*
16   *hopelessly romantic, foppish poet, calls on Louise to inquire*
17   *about the vacant room ... and the chase is on!*
18
19   **LOUISE:** My husband is not back yet.
20   **VERSATI:** You must have some authority.
21   **LOUISE:** Would you like to know the rate?
22   **VERSATI:** No.
23   **LOUISE:** Oh. Would you like to see the room?
24   **VERSATI:** That's not necessary.
25   **LOUISE:** You would rent a room without seeing it?
26   **VERSATI:** Yes.
27   **LOUISE:** Why?
28   **VERSATI:** Because ... because ... *(Blurts it out)* **Your**
29   **underpants!**

1　LOUISE: *(Shocked)* Oh my god! Who are you?
2　VERSATI: I am a poet. Unpublished — I am proud to say —
3　　but one who has now found his muse.
4　LOUISE: Please!
5　VERSATI: I will explain. By metaphor. No, by simile. No, I
6　　will not beat around the bush. Oh my god, what an
7　　inappropriate allusion. I am not the master of my soul.
8　　Though a few hours ago I was. It seems I am engulfed by
9　　the rising tide of my own humors ... *(He is pleased by his*
10　　*metaphor.)* What a beautiful line ... where is my pen! *(He*
11　　*can't find it.)* Damn. Society's loss. *(Back to her)* You see,
12　　I believe in miracles, and I finally had one appear to me
13　　under a linden tree. There you were, bathed in sunlight,
14　　with panicked eyes and a quivering body and there I was,
15　　shaken by life. A momentous crossroads. In those few
16　　seconds, when you bent down and collected your
17　　underpants, you tore my heart from the things that I
18　　loved, and fixed it only on you. *(LOUISE is breathless.)* Ah,
19　　silence. Good. For silence is devotion. *(He moves toward*
20　　*her.)*
21　LOUISE: I ... I ... don't know what to say.
22　VERSATI: Then let me speak: From this day on, I will desire
23　　you with all the strength of my soul. Unwavering,
24　　disavowing all others.
25　LOUISE: Please stand up.
26　VERSATI: I cannot stand, for my veins are stiff with
27　　certainty.
28　LOUISE: For god's sake, if my husband comes!
29　VERSATI: The room you have for rent. How much is it?
30　LOUISE: Fifteen taler.
31　VERSATI: I'll take it. The discussion is over.
32　LOUISE: Who would believe an elegant gentleman living in
33　　the neighborhood?
34　VERSATI: I'll dress as a laborer. A wealthy, gentleman hod
35　　carrier.

1 LOUISE: And you would live here?
2 VERSATI: In the extra room.
3 LOUISE: What about my husband?
4 VERSATI: If he comes, just introduce us. I'm renting the
5   room.
6 LOUISE: And you are ...?
7 VERSATI: Versati. Franklin, Angelo, "The Cat," Luigi,
8   Versati the second. Sorry, the third.
9 LOUISE: You should get up. He'll be coming back soon.
10 VERSATI: Between the sound of his key in the lock and the
11   opening of the door I will be fleet like Jupiter. Wait,
12   Jupiter is not fleet. Make that Mercury.
13 LOUISE: Get up!
14 VERSATI: You'll agree, then?
15 LOUISE: I ... *(They play the pause.)*
16 VERSATI: In the ellipsis sounds a yes!
17 LOUISE: But my husband?
18 VERSATI: Think of him as a necessary part of the triangle.
19   You are the flint, I am the fire, and he is the wet piece of
20   wood. I'll be back.

Supermarket Checkout
by Dina Gregory

1   *Two "friendly" but naughty neighbors — one large and the*
2   *other small — are pushing their shopping carts in a local*
3   *supermarket when they spot a man they know at the*
4   *checkout counter. The neighbors charge ahead and, after a*
5   *short chase, corner the bewildered man with their carts before*
6   *he can escape. The neighbors then bombard the now*
7   *speechless hostage with an unremitting fireworks display of*
8   *exploding clichés, puns, and meaningless catch phrases. The*
9   *chaotic scene resembles a blindfolded jigsaw-puzzle party in*
10   *which most of the pieces that might explain this bizarre*
11   *situation simply do not fit ... or are missing. Beneath the*
12   *obvious broad humor and comic confusion, there is a flavor*
13   *of the absurd here that only serves to heighten the mystery*
14   *of how to decode the true meaning of the actions and words.*
15
16   LARGE NEIGHBOR: We heard the bad news.
17   SMALL NEIGHBOR: You poor thing. Rotten luck!
18   LARGE NEIGHBOR: We won't mention it if you're still
19   sore —
20   SMALL NEIGHBOR: — Well, of course you are. How could
21   you not be?
22   LARGE NEIGHBOR: Never mind. It wasn't your fault.
23   SMALL NEIGHBOR: And even if it was, no point blaming
24   yourself, is there?
25   LARGE NEIGHBOR: What's done is done.
26   SMALL NEIGHBOR: Just a little glitch.
27   LARGE NEIGHBOR: A small hitch.
28   SMALL NEIGHBOR: A slight hiccup.
29   LARGE NEIGHBOR: No great belch.

1 SMALL NEIGHBOR: You win some, you lose some. Right?
2 Life is a learning curve.
3 LARGE NEIGHBOR: For some it tends towards the vertical,
4 that's all.
5 SMALL NEIGHBOR: Best to get on with things. Pick
6 yourself up and dust yourself off.
7 LARGE NEIGHBOR: You've still got your hands!
8 SMALL NEIGHBOR: I mean it really is a pity. But what can
9 you do? No point crying over spilled milk is there?
10 LARGE NEIGHBOR: Best to just mop it up and squeeze it
11 out — before it smells.
12 SMALL NEIGHBOR: We're always here for you. You know
13 that.
14 LARGE NEIGHBOR: Of course you know that.
15 SMALL NEIGHBOR: And anyway, you have to tumble before
16 you can fall.
17 LARGE NEIGHBOR: *(Quietly)* No, that's not it.
18 SMALL NEIGHBOR: *(Flustered)* Stumble before you can
19 tumble.
20 LARGE NEIGHBOR: Fall before you can —
21 SMALL NEIGHBOR: Crawl!
22 LARGE NEIGHBOR: Chew before you can ...
23 SMALL NEIGHBOR: Swallow?
24 LARGE NEIGHBOR: Eat the bitter with the ...
25 SMALL NEIGHBOR: Meat — sweet. *(Awkward pause)*
26 LARGE NEIGHBOR: *(Taking control)* The bottom line is
27 everyone makes mistakes.
28 SMALL NEIGHBOR: Some just make them more often.
29 LARGE NEIGHBOR: On a larger scale.
30 SMALL NEIGHBOR: Not that yours was big by any means.
31 LARGE NEIGHBOR: No, no. Very small.
32 SMALL NEIGHBOR: A mere trifle.
33 LARGE NEIGHBOR: Miniscule.
34 SMALL NEIGHBOR: Teeny-weeny.
35 LARGE NEIGHBOR: Hardly worth dwelling on.

1   SMALL NEIGHBOR: But we understand the disappointment.

2   LARGE NEIGHBOR: Your disappointment.

3   SMALL NEIGHBOR: Still, can't have everything your way.

4   LARGE NEIGHBOR: Like it or not, life isn't fair.

5   SMALL NEIGHBOR: It just isn't.

6   LARGE NEIGHBOR: Some are born to succeed. And some

7   aren't.

8   SMALL NEIGHBOR: They're just not.

9   LARGE NEIGHBOR: You're a born loser, that's all.

10   SMALL NEIGHBOR: One of life's little failures.

11   LARGE NEIGHBOR: Not even a spectacular one in the

12   grand scheme of things.

13   SMALL NEIGHBOR: Rather unremarkable.

14   LARGE NEIGHBOR: Really very ordinary. But you did your

15   best. And that's what counts.

16   SMALL NEIGHBOR: It doesn't add up to much. But it

17   counts.

18   LARGE NEIGHBOR: We're still behind you.

19   SMALL NEIGHBOR: All the way. One hundred percent.

20   LARGE NEIGHBOR: Just put this down to experience.

21   SMALL NEIGHBOR: A bad experience.

22   LARGE NEIGHBOR: A blunder.

23   SMALL NEIGHBOR: A boo-boo. *(Gets the giggles.)*

24   LARGE NEIGHBOR: You just made a mess of everything.

25   That's all. *(She gets the giggles too.)* Sorry but it's true.

26   *(They infect each other with hysteria.)*

27   SMALL NEIGHBOR: You botched things. Big time.

28   LARGE and SMALL NEIGHBORS: *(Both crying with laughter)*

29   You're a screw up!

Legal Acknowledgments

Copyright Caution

Copyright laws exist to protect the artistic and intellectual property rights of creators of original works. All creative works, such as theatre scripts, are considered copyrighted. There are, however, a number of "fair use" exceptions for educational or instructional purposes related to classroom performance. The scripts in this collection are fully protected under the copyright laws of the United States, the British Empire, the Dominion of Canada, and all other countries of the Copyright Union. For additional information related to full-scale production or other available scripts, please contact the author or the author's agent at the address listed.

Chapter 1: Reflections in the Mirror

"Beth," from *Blind Dog* by Tom Coash, Copyright©2006 by Tom Coash. Reprinted by permission of the author. For additional information please contact the author at thomascoash@sbcglobal.net.

"Kelly," by Shirley King. Copyright©2006 by Shirley King. Reprinted by permission of the author. For additional information please contact the author at sak934@aol.com or at P. O. Box 1034, Benicia, California 94510.

"Teenager," from "Paranoid" in *Power Pieces for Women* by Deborah Maddox. Copyright©2003 by Deborah Maddox. Reprinted by permission of the author and Lucid Solutions publishers. For additional information please contact the publishers at Lucid Solutions, P. O. Box 32141, Mesa, Arizona 85275.

"Woman," from "Alone In the Crowd" in *Eve's Daughters* by Gail Blanton. Copyright©2002 by Gail Blanton. Reprinted by permission of the author and Lillenas Publishing Company. All print rights administered by Lillenas Publishing Company. For additional information please contact the publisher at Lillenas Publishing Company, P. O. Box 419527, Kansas City, Missouri 64141 or at drama@lillenas.com.

"Carol," from *Walking Sideways* by Ruth McKee. Copyright©2005 by Ruth McKee. Reprinted by permission of the author. For additional information please contact the author at 853 Larrabel Street, #3, West Hollywood, California 90069 or at RuthAMckee@aol.com.

Chapter 2: Through the Looking Glass

"Brooke," from *Acceptance Speech* by Deanna Riley. Copyright©2006 by Deanna Riley. Reprinted by permission of the author. For additional information please contact the author at 8 Wayne Drive, Wilmington, Delaware 19809 or at deannarc@aol.com

"Gloria," from *Skylar* by Samara Siskind. Copyright©2006 by Samara Siskind. Reprinted by permission of the author. For additional information please contact the author's agent Buddy Thomas at International Creative Management, 825 Eighth Avenue, 26th Floor, New York, New York 10019.

"Young Girl," from *Raccoon Ball* by Jeff Goode. Copyright©2005 by Jeff Goode. Reprinted by permission of the author. For additional information please contact the author at www.JeffGoode@aol.com.

"Alyssa," from *Running Giraffe* by Laura E. Cotton. Copyright©2006 by Laura E. Cotton. Reprinted by permission of the author. For additional information please contact the author at 120 White Drive, Apt. D-32, Tallahassee, Florida 32304 or at savvyscreenwriter@hotmail.com.

"Chloe," from "Nuts" in *The Food Monologues* by Kerri Kochanski. Copyright©2005 by Kerri Kochanski. Reprinted by permission of the author. For additional information please contact the author at kerrikochanski@optonline.net.

"Teenager," from "Murder to What Degree?" in *Power Pieces for Women* by Deborah Maddox. Copyright©2003 by Deborah Maddox. Reprinted by permission of the author and Lucid Solutions publishers. For additional information please contact the publishers at Lucid Solutions, P. O. Box 32141, Mesa, Arizona 85275.

Chapter 3: Comic Mirrors

"Vicki Kearney," from *The Pyre* by Terri Campion. Copyright©2002 by Terri Campion. Reprinted by permission of the author. For additional information please contact the author at tarriecamp@aol.com.

"Francine," from "Women Alone" In *Heart Speak* by Christopher Woods. Copyright©2002 by Christopher Woods. Reprinted by permission of the author. For additional information please contact the author at dreamwood77019@hotmail.com.

"Loretta," from *Don't Call Me Loretta* by Nancy Gall-Clayton. Copyright©2004 by Nancy Gall-Clayton. For additional information please contact the author at nancygallclayton@earthlink.net.

Chapter 4: Cracked Mirrors

"Aleah," from the musical *Runaway Home* by Darren J. Butler. Copyright©2006 by Darren J. Butler. Book and lyrics by Darren J. Butler. Lyrics and music by Judy Rodman and Will Fincher. Reprinted by permission of the author. For additional information please contact the author at 916 Tracey Lane, S.W., Decatur, Alabama 35601 or at darrenjbutler@aol.com.

"Kristen," from *Bridewell* by Charles Evered. Copyright©2002 by Charles Evered. Reprinted by permission of the author. For additional information please contact the author at 94 Leigh Avenue, Princeton, New Jersey 08542 or at CBEvered@aol.com.

"Woman," from "Dead" in *Funnylogues for Women* by Mort Kaufman, Roger Karshner, and Zelda Abel. Copyright©2004 by Mort Kaufman, Roger Karshner, and Zelda Abel. Reprinted by permission of the authors and Dramaline Publications, LLC. For additional information please contact the publisher at Dramaline Publications, LCC.. 36-851 Palm View Road, Rancho Mirage, California 92270 or at drama.line@verizon.net.

"Ms. Grinch," from *What Is Gained: A Muse on Consequence* by Evan Guilford-Blake. Copyright©2006 by Evan Guilford-Blake. Adapted from the author's full-length script *True Magic*. Reprinted by permission of the author. For additional information please contact the author at ejbplaywright@yahoo.com.

"Marcella," from *Happy Endings* by Judith Hancock. Copyright©2002 by Judith Hancock. Reprinted by permission of the author. For additional information please contact the author at jdonnerh@rcn.com.

"Genny," from "Bones" in *The Food Monologues* by Kerri Kochanski. Copyright©2004 by Kerri Kochanski. Reprinted by permission of the author. For additional information please contact the author at kerrikochanski@optonline.net.

"Chris," from *Bedside Manners* by Lisa Stephenson. Copyright©2004 by Lisa Stephenson. Reprinted by permission of the author. For additional information please contact the author at 2401 Ingleside Avenue, #10B, Cincinnati, Ohio 45206 or at ZT@fuse.net.

"Mari," from *Cleveland Raining* by Sung Rno. Copyright©2003 by Sung Rno. Reprinted by permission of the author and Bret Adams Ltd. For additional information please contact Bret Adams Ltd., 448 W. 44th Street, New York, New York 10036.

"Alice," from *Epiphany Cake* by Kelly Younger. Copyright©2004 by Kelly Younger. Reprinted by permission of the author. For additional information please contact the author at kyounger@lmu.edu.

"Brenda Pinto," from "Cocktail Hour at Gibson Southern High School's Tenth Year Reunion" in *Swinging For the Fences* by Elizabeth Dembrowsky. Copyright©2006 by Elizabeth Dembrowsky. Reprinted by permission of the author. For additional information please contact the author at 30-37 49th Street, #2N, Astoria, New York 11103 or at dembrowskaya@yahoo.com.

"Woman," from *It Doesn't Take a Tornado* by Rosanna Yamagiwa Alfaro. Copyright©2005 by Rosanna Yamagiwa Alfaro. Reprinted by permission of the author and Heinemann Publishers. All reproduction and performance privileges are prohibited without prior written permission of the author. For additional information please contact the author at 10 Appian Way, Cambridge, Massachusetts 02138.

"Cece," from *Squats* by Martin Jones. Copyright©2005 by Martin Jones. Reprinted by permission of the author. For additional information please contact the author at 830 E. Delmar Street, Springfield, Missouri 65807 or at rmartinjones@mchsi.com.

"Fran," from "Anorexia" in *Hunger* by Peter Langman. Copyright©2006 by Peter Langman. Reprinted by permission of the author. For additional information please contact the author at peterlangman@ yahoo.com.

Chapter 5: Stained Mirrors

"Ms. Smith," from *She Must Like It* by Tom Coash. Copyright©2006 by Tom Coash. Reprinted by permission of the author. For additional information please contact the author at thomascoash@sbcglobal.net.

"Peggy," from *Big Girl* by Andrew Biss. Copyright©2005 by Andrew Biss. Reprinted by permission of the author. For additional information please contact the author at andrewbiss@earthlink.net.

"Ruby," from *King Hedley II* in *The Fire This Time: African American Plays for the 21st Century* by August Wilson. Copyright©1994 by August Wilson. Published by Theatre Communications Group. Reprinted by permission of Theatre Communications Group. For additional information please contact the publisher at Theatre Communications Group, 520 8th Avenue, 24th Floor, New York, New York 10018.

Chapter 6: Shattered Mirrors

Chapter 7: Mirror Images

Elephants and Coffee by Aoise Stratford. Copyright©2002 by Aoise Stratford. Reprinted by permission of the author. For additional information please contact the author at aoise@hotmail.com or at www.aoisestratford.com.

"Ah, Shucks!" from *Wait a Minute!* by Edward Crosby Wells. Copyright©2006 by Edward Crosby Wells. Reprinted by permission of the author. For additional information please contact the author at edwardcrosbywells@yahoo.com.

"Boy Meets Girl," from *Bachelor Girls* by Wendy Wasserstein. Copyright©1990 by Wendy Wasserstein. Reprinted by permission of Alfred A. Knopf, a division of Random House, Inc. For more information please contact the publisher at Random House, Inc., 1745 Broadway, New York, New York 10019.

Stolen Identity by Steve Ghent. Copyright©2006 by Steve Ghent. Reprinted by permission of the author. For additional information please contact the author at 2783 New South Drive, Marietta, Georgia 30066 or at sghent@hotmail/.com.

The Last Yankee by Arthur Miller. Copyright©2004 by Arthur Miller Literary and Dramatic Property Trust. Reprinted by permission of International Creative Management, Inc. For additional information please contact International Creative Management, Inc., 40 West 57th Street, New York, New York 10019.

Frailty, Thy Name Is Woe by Paddy Gillard Bentley. Copyright©2003 by Paddy Gillard Bentley. Reprinted by permission of the author. For additional information please contact the author at 24 Wellington Street N., Kitchener, Ontario, N2H 5J4, Canada or at paddy@skyedragon.com.

The Underpants by Carl Sternheim. Adapted by Steve Martin. Copyright©2002 by 40 Share Productions. Reprinted by permission of Hyperion. All rights reserved. For additional information please contact Hyperion, 77 W. 66th Street, 11th Floor, New York, New York 10023.

"Supermarket Checkout," from *Spitting Distance* by Diana Gregory. Copyright©2005 by Diana Gregory. Reprinted by permission of the author. For additional information please contact the author at sorayagregory@gmail.com.

Supplementary Resource Materials

The following resource materials are recommended for those who wish to become better acquainted with additional sources of competitive monologues, new playscripts, basic audition terminology, and summer career opportunities. The resource materials represent a sample of current theatre practices and may be especially useful in identifying texts and theatre directories. Useful information also includes valuable references related to audition tips and placement agencies at both the regional and national level.

Basic Audition Terminology

Bit: Small piece of stage business used in blocking.

Blocking: Pictorial composition of actors' movements to create "stage pictures" that illustrate dramatic action of the text.

Business: Small piece of action used in blocking.

Call Time: Expected arrival time at audition, rehearsal, or performance.

Cheat: Moving one's body or face slightly out toward auditorium house; slight adjustment in movement in any direction to focus or balance stage picture.

Closed Audition: Only actors invited to attend may audition.

Counter: Moving in opposite direction from another actor to balance stage picture.

Cross: Physically moving on-stage from one place to another.

Cue: Action or dialogue that signals next business, dialogue, or movement that follows.

Find the Light: Locate place on-stage where lights have been focused or place where best available stage light is located.

French Scene: Break-down of script into smaller scenes for rehearsal.

General Audition: Monologues prepared in advance by actors; memorized and blocked to demonstrate individual ability rather than an audition for a specific character role.

Give Stage: Change stage position to permit focus or emphasis on another actor.

Inner Life: Character's personal philosophy, point of view, and individual personality.

Off Book: Having lines of dialogue memorized and able to perform without text in hand.

Open Audition: All interested actors, amateur or professional, are encouraged to attend and audition.

Over Play: Giving action, dialogue, or movement more emphasis or exaggeration than required.

Pick Up Cues: Leaving no pause or blank space between previous actor's last line of dialogue and beginning of next line of dialogue.

Play Up (Plug or Punch): Emphasize key line, movement, or stage business for greater significance.

Shtick: Bits of comic stage business.

Sides: Photocopied pages of selected scenes or individual character speeches to be read at auditions.

Steal: Actor drawing attention away from a character to whom emphasis would normally be directed in the given circumstances of the text.

Tag Line: Final spoken line of dialogue when exiting stage.

Take Stage: Actor assumes a more prominent body position or moves to more prominent stage area to gain focus or emphasis.

Throw Away: To deliberately underplay or de-emphasize a line of dialogue or stage business to re-direct focus or attention elsewhere.

Top: Additional emphasis given to a line of dialogue or an action that is more emphatic than the line of dialogue or stage business that precedes it.

Monologues and New Theatre Scripts

Good sources for the acting edition of a script and for texts by new playwrights.

Pioneer Drama Service
PO Box 4267
Englewood, CO 80155-4267
www.pioneerdrama.com

Samuel French, Inc.
45 West 25th Street
New York, NY 10010
(212) 206-8990
www.samuelfrench.com

Theatre Communications Group
520 8th Avenue
24th Floor
New York, NY 10018
tcg@tcg.org

Internet Public Library
Online Texts Collection
www.ipl.org

Dramatists Play Service
440 Park Avenue South
New York, NY 10016
(212) 683-8960
www.dramatists.com

Playscripts, Inc.
325 West 38th Street
Suite 305
New York, NY 10018
www.playscripts.com

Internet Theatre Bookshop
Catalog of Playscripts
stageplays.com

Theatre Texts and Audition Tips

Actor Tips
Audition Hints
info@actortips.com

Summer Theatre 2007
PO Box 159
Dorset, VT 05251

Theatre Web Resources
Virtual Library
vl-theatre.com

Artslynx International
Online Theatre Resources
rfinkelso@msn.com

Moonstruck Drama Bookstore
New Playscripts
newdrama@aol.com

Backstage
The Actor's Resource
www.backstage.com

Theatre Directories and Arts Agencies

Dramatists Guild
1501 Broadway
Suite 701
New York, NY 10036

The Playwrights Center
2301 Frankline Avenue, E.
Minneapolis, MN 55406

Writers & Artists
19 W. 44th Street
Suite 1000
New York, NY 10036

New Dramatists
424 W. 44th Street
New York, NY 10036

Educational Theatre Association
Teaching Resources
www.etassoc.org

Dramatics Magazine
2343 Auburn Avenue
Cincinnati, OH 45219

Career Opportunities

Astroworld (Six Flags)
9001 Kirby Drive
Houston, TX 77054
(713) 794-3232

Disneyland
PO Box 3232
Anaheim, CA 92803
(714) 781-3445

Dollywood
1020 Dollywood Lane
Pigeon Forge, TN 37863
(423) 428-9433

Hershey Park
100 West Hershey Park Drive
Hersey, PA 17033
(717) 534-3336

Paramount's King's Island
6300 King's Island Drive
King's Island, OH 45034
(513) 573-5740

Busch Gardens Williamsburg
One Busch Gardens Boulevard
Williamsburg, VA 23187
(757) 253-3302

About the Editor

Gerald Lee Ratliff is the award-winning author of numerous articles, essays, and textbooks in performance studies and classroom teaching strategies. He has served as President of the Speech and Theatre Association of New Jersey (1983), Eastern Communication Association (1991), Theta Alpha Phi (1986), and the Association for Communication Administration (2002). He has also served on advisory and editorial boards of the American Council of Academic Deans, International Arts Association, National Communication Association, Society of Educators and Scholars, and Eastern Communication Association.

He was awarded the "Distinguished Service Award" by both the Eastern Communication Association (1993) and Theta Alpha Phi (1992); named a Fulbright Scholar to China (1990); selected as U.S.A. delegate of the John F. Kennedy Center for the Performing Arts to Russia (1991); received multiple outstanding teacher awards for pioneering creative approaches in curriculum design and classroom instruction activities; and chaired a number of national commissions in higher education. Most recently, he was named Educator of the Year (2003) by the International Biographical Centre in Cambridge, England, and awarded the prestigious da Vinci Diamond for his contribution to national and international associations.

In addition, he has served as a program consultant and planner for a number of colleges and universities engaged in institutional transformation. He also continues an active schedule of invited workshops and seminars in Reader's Theatre at high schools, colleges, universities, and national conferences. For additional information, please contact him at ratlifgl@potsdam.edu or at (315) 267-2107.